M000086553

JOINING JESUS ON THE WAY

JOINING JESUS ON THE WAY

Discipleship in the 21st Century

Phil Mayo

ELM HILL

A Division of
HarperCollins Christian Publishing

www.elmhillbooks.com

© 2019 Phil Mayo

Joining Jesus on the Way

Discipleship in the 21st Century

All rights reserved. No portion of this book may be reproduced, stored in a retrieval system, or transmitted in any form or by any means—electronic, mechanical, photocopy, recording, scanning, or other—except for brief quotations in critical reviews or articles, without the prior written permission of the publisher.

Published in Nashville, Tennessee, by Elm Hill, an imprint of Thomas Nelson. Elm Hill and Thomas Nelson are registered trademarks of HarperCollins Christian Publishing, Inc.

Elm Hill titles may be purchased in bulk for educational, business, fund-raising, or sales promotional use. For information, please e-mail SpecialMarkets@ ThomasNelson.com.

All Scripture quotations, unless otherwise indicated, are taken from the Holy Bible, New International Version', NIV'. Copyright © 1973, 1978, 1984, 2011 by Biblica, Inc.' Used by permission of Zondervan. All rights reserved worldwide. www.Zondervan. com. The "NIV" and "New International Version" are trademarks registered in the United States Patent and Trademark Office by Biblica, Inc.'

Scripture quotations marked KJV are from the King James Version. Public domain.

Scripture quotations marked TNIV are from the Holy Bible, Today's New International' Version TNIV'. Copyright 2001, 2005 by International Bible Society'. Used by permission of International Bible Society'. All rights reserved worldwide. "TNIV" and "Today's New International Version" are trademarks registered in the United States Patent and Trademark Office by International Bible Society'.

Library of Congress Cataloging-in-Publication Data

Library of Congress Control Number: 2019911135

ISBN 978-1-400328123 (Paperback)
ISBN 978-1-400328130 (eBook)

To my dad
My first teacher

TABLE OF CONTENTS

ABBREVIATIONS

EJ	Enrichment Journal
NTL	The New Testament Library
NINTC	New International New Testament Commentary
NT	New Testament
OT	Old Testament
SOM	Sermon on the Mount
SOP	Sermon on the Plain

ACKNOWLEDGMENTS

This book, like most books, began as a dream about three years ago. I have always desired to write a book that would be of service to the church in a much broader way than the academic writing I have done. Like all dreams, this one did not come about without hard work and a lot of help from many people. So, I would like to offer a few words of thanks to those who have helped this book become a reality.

First of all, I would like to thank the administration of North Central University who granted me a yearlong sabbatical in order to write this book. The time to reflect and to write has been invaluable. I would also like to thank my colleagues at North Central who have encouraged and cheered me along the way. A special thanks goes to Dr. Leslie Evens, Professor of English at North Central University, for reading portions of the manuscript and offering style, grammar, and punctuation suggestions. I, however, bear the full responsibility for the final product and any errors that remain.

My family, as well, have been a tremendous support to me throughout this process. Mark Kamleiter, my brother-in-law, read portions of the manuscript and offered a number of helpful suggestions. He and his wife, my sister Julia, as well as my sister Karen encouraged me, prayed for me, and supported me in every way possible. I am deeply indebted to their love.

My wife Jolene has been my rock. She has read each chapter throughout the process of writing and thinks everything I write is wonderful. Every writer needs someone like her. I couldn't have done any of this without her support, trust, love, and prayers. She is a gift from God, and her presence reminds me every day of God's love. Finally, to God be all the glory for the inspiration and for the fruit that might be borne as a result of this work.

INTRODUCTION

THE JOURNEY BEGINS

L uke is my favorite Gospel. Of course, as I have often told my students over the years, picking your favorite book in the Bible is much like trying to pick your favorite piece of chocolate out of a box of chocolates. They are all good, but some appeal to you more than others! Luke is that kind of Gospel for me. One reason I love his writings, in general, is that Luke doesn't leave us wondering what happened after Jesus ascended into heaven. After all, Jesus chose and invested himself into at least twelve disciples, and it is nice to know that they actually lived up to the call he placed on their lives. We can look at the church today and our own personal faith to know that they didn't fail, and the letters of Paul certainly affirm that as well. However, Luke does us the favor of giving us a sequel to his Gospel—the book of Acts—which documents key moments in the lives and activities of the early believers as they move out from Jerusalem unto the uttermost parts of the earth.

I love Luke's Gospel, too, because it is likely written by a Gentile. I say "likely" because we don't know this for certain. A handful of scholars argue that Luke is a Jew. It is true that he is very familiar with Jewish customs and the Jewish Scriptures, at least the Greek translation of them known as the Septuagint (LXX). However, Colossians 4.10–14 tends to suggest that Luke is among the gentile companions of Paul. I think he

1

is probably a God-fearer. These are Gentiles who were attracted to the monotheism of the Jews, the righteous living required by the Law, but never fully proselytized. Luke tends to highlight these Gentiles in Acts; the Centurion Cornelius in Acts 10 is an example. Luke himself was probably one among their number and received the message of salvation through Jesus with great joy and became an active companion of Paul on his journeys.

All of this means that Luke is not an original follower of Jesus. Where he is from or how he heard the gospel message is the subject of speculation. If the "we" passages in the book of Acts[1] are to be taken as eyewitness accounts of the author, and they should be, then the first time we meet Luke in Acts is when he joins Paul's mission in Philippi. Some have speculated that Luke comes from Philippi, especially since a first-century medical school was located there.[2] Others have suggested that he originated in Antioch, but no one really knows. Since our first encounter with Luke through the "we" passages in Acts takes place in Philippi (Acts 16.11), it is possible that he is a convert of Paul's ministry there. Whatever the case, he certainly became a "beloved" companion and partner of Paul (Col 4.14).

The Uniqueness of Luke

I like Luke's writing because Luke is well-educated, and his writing reflects his skill. Luke writes in the accepted style for historians of his day, and his command of Greek means that his works reflect some of the best in the New Testament. Both of his works begin with a prologue, what we might call a preface today, with the Gospel preface being the longer of the two. In the preface to the Gospel, he outlines his reason for writing and that he has "carefully investigated" those things handed down from the "eyewitnesses and servants of the word" (Lk 1.1–2). Luke is a careful historian, and throughout Luke-Acts, he provides historical markers for the events that happen, showing that God is fulfilling his promises in full view of humanity. As Paul tells King Agrippa, "It was not done in a corner" (Acts 26.26).

Luke also writes with purpose. Not only does his preface reflect his intentions, but the flow of the narrative throughout Luke-Acts, and the consistent development of key themes, demonstrates that he has clear understanding of his literary intent and carries it out with singular purpose. The way we discern Luke's themes and intent is by noting how stories are placed together, the details that are and are not included, the details that are emphasized over others, and what unique material is present. In order to discern all of these things, we must have other similar works to which we can compare Luke's.

We are blessed to have three other Gospels, two of which have many of the same stories as Luke. These other two, Matthew and Mark, along with Luke, are called the Synoptic Gospels. Synoptic means "a seeing together," and this happens with these three Gospels. They, together, present us with a similar view of who Jesus is. By looking at these Gospels side by side, we can notice subtle and not-so-subtle differences in the way they present Jesus's life and ministry that reveal their unique themes and theological emphases. We might call these differences their "literary fingerprints." To be sure, all three Gospels (all four for that matter) present Jesus as the Son of God and the Savior of the world, but the way they do that is what interests us. I hope that in the next few chapters, we can "dust for these fingerprints" and watch emerge from the pages of Luke's writings his unique perspective.

The Travel Narrative

The literary theme that most interests us for the present discussion is discipleship. It has long been recognized that the teachings of Jesus in Luke's Gospel are most often directed to his disciples, even though a much larger crowd may be looming in the background. Perhaps this emphasis on the disciples' training is to prepare for the presentation of Jesus's continued ministry through these same followers in Luke's second volume, Acts.[3] Most of this discipleship material is contained in the section of the Gospel known as the "travel narrative," which begins in

3

Luke 9.51 and extends through the triumphal entry into Jerusalem, which ends in 19.44. As we can see, the travel narrative is a large portion of the Gospel, about ten chapters of the twenty-four, and gets its name from the literary motif around which this portion of the Gospel is written—Jesus's journey up to Jerusalem.

Luke introduces the travel narrative very intentionally. He states that "as the time approached for [Jesus] to be taken up to heaven," Jesus set his face "resolutely" toward Jerusalem (9.51). So, it is here that Jesus begins to ascend from Galilee up to the Holy City. Most scholars recognize that this travel narrative does not make much geographical sense, if Luke intended it to be taken literally. For example, before Jesus's encounter with ten lepers in chapter seventeen, Luke provides us with a geographical marker; he writes, "Now on his way to Jerusalem, Jesus traveled along the border between Samaria and Galilee" (17.11). Jesus had begun his journey in 9.51 and in the following verses, 9.52–53, is already passing through Samaritan villages, one of which refuses him hospitality. Yet, about two-thirds of the way through the travel narrative, Jesus is still no closer to Jerusalem! This confusion is not an indicator that Luke is geographically challenged, but that this journey is more than just a log of Jesus's travels up to Jerusalem. It is a motif on which Luke can hang Jesus's teaching and around which Luke can convey, among other things, the theme of discipleship.

All of this begs the question as to why Luke chooses a traveling theme to present the majority of Jesus's discipleship teaching. In brief, I think the answer is twofold. First, Luke recognizes that discipleship is a journey on which we walk side by side with the Master, as he not only instructs us but also reveals himself to us. Second, Jesus is on the way to the cross in his journey, and he invites every disciple on this journey. We must die to ourselves in order to truly live with him. This is what it means to take up the cross and to deny ourselves. These things are not easily understood and are counterintuitive to our human nature, so the Master walks with us and demonstrates the way to true life and peace in him.

This journey motif connects also with Acts through Luke's numerous references to Christianity as "the Way" (Acts 9.2; 19.9; 19.23; 24.22). Speculation suggests that Luke has in mind Isaiah 35 where the prophet speaks of the joy of God's future redemption. In this passage the prophet speaks of a highway that "will be called *the Way* of Holiness; it will be for those who walk on *that Way*... only *the redeemed will walk there*" (Isa 35:8–9 italics mine).

If this passage is not in view, Isa 40.3–5 certainly is. Luke declares the fulfillment of this passage at the beginning of John the Baptist's ministry (Lk 3.4–6). Isaiah writes, "Comfort, comfort my people, says your God. Speak tenderly to Jerusalem, and proclaim to her that her hard service has been completed, that her sin has been paid for, that she has received from the Lord's hand double for all her sins" (40.1–2). This is a prophecy of hope, of the return of God's favor on his people, and is a messianic prophecy. The Lord is coming and will visit his people, so Isaiah says "prepare *the way* of the Lord" (40.3 italics mine). John the Baptist is that voice calling in the wilderness, calling the people back to God through a baptism of repentance for the remission of sins.

At the end of his Gospel, Luke records two resurrection appearances of Jesus, one of which is particularly unique to his Gospel. Two of Jesus's disciples are traveling from Jerusalem to Emmaus when the resurrected Jesus joins them on the way (24.35). Unrecognized by them, Jesus begins to show them how he has fulfilled all that was written about him in the Scriptures. At the end of the journey, he reveals himself to them during the breaking of bread and then disappears from their sight.

Discipleship according to Luke, then, is a journey on which we are invited to join Jesus on the way to the cross, and on this journey Jesus is revealed to us. We must not despair, however, because just beyond the cross is the resurrection to new life in him.

Every true disciple of Jesus desires a revelation of him, but that revelation must come on a journey that first begins with an encounter with the risen Lord and requires a commitment like no other. Luke has a unique understanding of the requirements of being a disciple, because he not only became one, but he also carefully investigated Jesus's teaching on discipleship and watched those teachings lived out in the lives of the early believers. Like Jesus, the early disciples lived out the kingdom principles he taught with undying commitment. Their selfless leadership spread the good news of the kingdom throughout the known world and left a lasting heritage for the millions who would follow.

Why Discipleship?

I completed a PhD program in 2004 and began teaching the Bible at the university level that year. I love teaching and studying the Scriptures. My love affair with the Bible really began as a teenager when I spent three years in Teen Bible Quiz through my church. Ever since then, I have spent years studying the Scriptures and have loved every minute of it. About three years ago, the idea for writing this book began to emerge.

I have taught Luke-Acts for many years and have grown to love Luke's Gospel. I learned and came to recognize myself his emphasis on discipleship and was fascinated with it. I also began to recognize a lack in my own spirituality. Some of the discipleship characteristics I saw in Jesus's teaching and being lived out in Acts weren't present in my life. I began to wonder, "What does it mean to 'take up your cross daily'"? "Sell your possessions and give to the poor." Really?! Why don't I see other people doing that? In America, I don't tend to see destitute Christians but mostly wealthy ones. In fact, in some of the circles I have traveled, some ministers and teachers make a theology out of being rich, as if that is what God intends for everyone. "Deny yourself," Jesus says. I'm not sure how all of this fits together!

These commands of Jesus challenged me, so I decided to investigate them. The result is this book. I recognize, of course, that this isn't the only book written on discipleship, but I think I offer a fresh perspective. As I indicated, a study of this topic is personal for me in that I desire to comprehend what it truly means to be a disciple of Jesus and to challenge myself in my faith walk to take a step closer to that "followship" to which Jesus calls me. I joined Jesus "on the way" over forty years ago, but, like the apostle Paul, "I press on to take hold of that for which Christ Jesus took hold of me" (Phil 3.12).

I have found myself in recent years questioning whether I really understand and have made the kind of commitment to following Christ that true discipleship demands. All believers are called to discipleship but not all answer that call. It's not always our fault, as we seem to hear very little these days about true discipleship. Some are answering the call but don't know what to do next. Their pursuit of Jesus is avid, but they need someone to help them along the way. It is my hope that this book will be that help.

What Jesus claims and to what he calls us often get lost in the church's message today. I have spent all of my life in the global West, mostly in the United States but also in Europe, so I think I have a pretty good handle on the ups and downs of at least the US Christian church. In the United States, we are all about inviting people to follow Jesus, but do we really know what that means? Being "seeker sensitive" is the buzzword today for orienting services toward people who are not part of the church but are maybe curious. It seems just another trend in the American church of creating more appeal to a gospel message that has perhaps fallen on hard times.

Once a person decides to follow Christ and to engage the church's invitation to join the community, what follows? What do we teach them about what it looks like to follow Jesus? What do we know about his seemingly radical claims? Do we encourage them, like Jesus did to his first would-be disciples, to count the cost? Do we really know what that cost is? Do we know what it means to take up our cross daily and follow him? Do we know what a life of faith, prayer, and giving up all means in the twenty-first century? The answers to these questions and many others are for me, personal, and for the greater contemporary church, vital. I believe that the power and resiliency of the end-time church rest in its complete devotion to the Master, who calls us to deny ourselves, take up the cross, and follow him.

In the following chapters, we will parse out what it means to join Jesus on the way and consider what discipleship looks like according to Luke. I believe that we will find that Jesus's call to discipleship is a call to join him on the way to the cross but will end with resurrection to a new life in him. In Chapter One, we will look at how discipleship begins through an encounter with Jesus. This encounter forces us to make a decision about Jesus's claims and whether we will accept his invitation to follow. In Chapter Two, we will consider the conditions of discipleship as Jesus tells his followers—unless you do these things, you "cannot be my disciple." Chapters Three and Four will deal, respectively, with disciples and their possessions and the need to listen to and obey the Master. Chapters Five and Six will cover the only two requests made by the disciples of Jesus in all of Luke, "Increase our faith" and "Lord, teach us to pray." Faith and prayer are vital for effective discipleship, as are the presence and power of the Holy Spirit, which is the subject of the last chapter, as well as the last of Jesus's commands to his disciples—"stay in the city until you have been clothed with power from on high" (Lk 24.49).

Writing this book has been a journey for me. I sensed in the beginning that studying these passages and the subject of discipleship would be as much (or more!) about my spiritual growth than that of others. That being said, I have written this book in hope that it will challenge others, and the greater church community, to deepen their walk with the Lord and to choose to take up that proverbial cross and follow him daily. I know it has done that for me, and I hope it will do the same for you.

1   Acts 16.10-17; 20.5-15; 21.1-18; 27.1-37; 28.1-16.

2   Ben Witherington III speculates on such a possibility in his commentary, *The Acts of the Apostles: A Socio-Rhetorical Commentary* (Grand Rapids: Eerdmans, 1998), 53, 490.

3   Luke Timothy Johnson makes this observation in his book, *Prophetic Jesus, Prophetic Church: The Challenge of Luke-Acts to Contemporary Christians* (Grand Rapids: Eerdmans, 2011).

CHAPTER ONE

AN ENCOUNTER

E ugene Peterson defines discipleship as "a long obedience in the same direction,"[1] which is a line he borrows from Friedrich Nietzsche's *Beyond Good and Evil*. There is certainly much truth to this description of discipleship, although Nietzsche was not talking about discipleship when he made this statement. I suppose this is a fundamental description of discipleship, but I think it is far more multidimensional than this. Peterson is correct, however, that if we are going to discuss discipleship, we should attempt to define or describe it in some manner. It is my hope that this book will meet that requirement, at least according to Luke. While this is certainly just one perspective, I think Luke's point of view is one of the fullest portrayed among the Gospels.

To begin, we can say that a disciple is simply a learner. In the ancient world, philosophers and Jewish rabbis usually had disciples. This is how they passed on their teachings and maintained their philosophical or religious schools. Disciples were typically young men who sat at the feet of the teacher and learned from him. While it was unusual in these very male-centered cultures to have female disciples, Jesus did. Even though he did not have any women among his chosen twelve, Luke tells us that he indeed had women among the larger entourage of devoted disciples who supported Jesus and the twelve (8.1–3). These women follow Jesus all the way from Galilee to Jerusalem, are present at the cross, and are the first eyewitnesses to the resurrection.

Jesus had a *lot* of people who followed him, but not everyone made the cut to be his disciple. I remember when I was in junior high and high school always being one of the last guys picked for team sports. I wasn't very athletic and was more of an academic. When I was in ninth grade, I developed a pretty strong interest in basketball and got pretty good at it. Being tall, it was a natural fit for me. In tenth grade, I decided, along with a good friend of mine, to try out for the junior varsity team. Tryouts were grueling, and I ultimately didn't make the first cut, so that was the end of my athletic career. Fortunately, being Jesus's disciple does not require innate talent or athletic ability, nor are there any "tryouts." It simply requires a willing heart.

Discipleship begins at the feet of Jesus, learning from him and then going and doing what he requires. I think this is why Jesus's feet figure prominently in Luke's Gospel. Peter, the "sinful woman" in Simon's house, and Mary, the sister of Martha, all find what they need at Jesus's feet. For Peter and the "sinful woman," it is the place of true repentance—it is the place where discipleship begins. For Mary, it is the place of learning—it is the place where discipleship continues.

I remember vividly my own first encounter with Jesus. I was fourteen years old, and my father had just suddenly and unexpectedly passed away. As a teenager, it was a world-shattering experience. I had worked closely with my dad and knew I would miss him. I had never encountered death so close-up and personal, and it truly rocked my world. My dad was a part-time pastor and a full-time businessman. He was not well educated, as he had to quit school in the seventh grade to work on the farm. But he had a lot of innate intelligence. He was part of what many now call "the greatest generation"—the one that was raised in the Great Depression and came of age during World War II. My dad went into the ministry later in life and never pastored churches that could pay him an adequate salary to care for his family of five children. So, he started out at the bottom of a local appliance business and worked his way up until he bought the business.

Being raised in a pastor's home meant that I was well acquainted with the gospel message and the importance of salvation through Jesus. While I always tried to be a good kid, I never really seemed to gain any traction as a believer. Sometimes growing up around the church and the gospel message is a disadvantage as constant exposure creates a narcotic effect that dulls the senses to the uniqueness and importance of the message. However, that all changed for me about three days after my father's passing. The world was different now, and death had suddenly become real.

Lying in bed one evening, a number of thoughts began to run through my mind. I remember distinctly becoming vividly aware of my own sin and need for a savior. It was like someone flipped a switch and a light came on. I can't explain why I felt this way, but I can only assume it was the result of a wooing from the Holy Spirit. I got out of bed and went into the family room where the rest of my family was sitting in conversation trying to make sense of the recent tragedy. I told them what I was feeling, and they all joyously knelt with me in prayer as I asked God for forgiveness and Christ into my life. I remember still how joyous and light I felt after that prayer, as if a burden had suddenly been lifted off my shoulders. I knew God, my Heavenly Father, had gently scooped me up in his arms and I had encountered the risen Savior. My journey with Jesus had begun, but it would be along the way that I would come to understand fully what true discipleship would look like.

This is the way that discipleship begins—with an encounter with Jesus and an opportunity to join Jesus on the journey. In Luke, encountering Jesus takes on a variety of forms. For Peter, James, and John, Jesus simply asked to borrow a boat. Sometimes Jesus asks us to give him what we have and he will make it more. For Mary Magdalene it was deliverance from the captivity of seven demons, and, similarly, for many others, it was such power encounters that drew them to follow Jesus (e.g., blind man at Jericho (Lk 18.43)). For Zacchaeus, it was a desperate need to see Jesus that gained him an invitation from Christ. For the three would-be disciples at the beginning of Jesus's journey to Jerusalem, discipleship was, for the two, a moment to volunteer and, for the third, an invitation from Jesus (9.57–62).

In Luke, Peter is the first of several disciples to receive an invitation to follow Jesus. Jesus is teaching a crowd along the shore of the Lake of Gennesaret[2] when he spots two boats along the water's edge. Since the crowd was pressing in on him, he climbed into the boat belonging to Simon Peter and asked him to push out a bit from the shore so he could teach the crowd. This kept the crowd from pressing in on Jesus and provided a natural amphitheater for him to be heard.

When Jesus finished teaching, he ordered Simon to put the boat out into deeper water in order to let down his nets for fish. Simon, having had a fruitless night at fishing, reluctantly did what Jesus said and caught such a great number of fish that their nets started to break and they had to call for help from their partners in the other boat. Peter's response to this miraculous catch was to fall at the knees of Jesus and to confess his sin. "Go away from me, Lord," he said, "for I am a sinful man!" (Lk 5.8). Jesus responded, "Don't be afraid; from now on you will fish for people" (Lk 5.10).

An Encounter Demands a Decision

Every encounter with Jesus elicits some kind of response. We both repent and recognize who he is or, like Simon the Pharisee in Luke 7, we fail to recognize in whose presence we stand (7.44–47). Luke tells us Peter's companions were also astonished at the catch of fish and, along with Peter, make the decision to leave everything and follow Jesus. Peter's partners, who joined him in discipleship, were none other than James and John, the sons of Zebedee. These three are destined to be Jesus's closest disciples and leaders of the fledgling group Jesus leaves behind to continue his work.

The encounter that Peter and his companions have with Jesus demonstrates a pattern of encounter portrayed throughout the Gospel of

Luke. Luke records several one-on-one encounters between Jesus and individuals in the Gospel all of whom are brought to a place where they must decide what they will do with Jesus. In fact, this decision theme is carried throughout beginning with Jesus's announcement of his ministry in Nazareth (Lk 4.14–30) through the crucifixion story (Lk 23.39-43).

In Luke 4, Luke sets side by side two stories of how people will ultimately respond to the claims of Jesus. In Nazareth, he is a prophet not accepted in his own country. Unable to see Jesus as other than "Joseph's son," the inhabitants of Nazareth ultimately become angry at his message and take him to the top of a cliff to throw him down. Yet, in the very next passage, Jesus is in Capernaum where he is able to heal many and the people marvel at his teaching. This bipolar response to Jesus's claims is really a fulfillment of what he says, "Do you think I came to bring peace on earth? No, I tell you, but division. From now on there will be five in one family divided against each other, three against two and two against three" (12.51–52). The division Jesus brings is a division that results from choice—a division between those who accept his message and those who do not.

The rich ruler (18.18–30) and the tax collector, Zacchaeus (19.1–10), are another example of contrasting responses. Both men are wealthy and have position, both approach Jesus on their own, and both have a personal encounter that forces them to make a discipleship decision. The rich ruler allows his wealth to keep him from joining Jesus on the way; but Zacchaeus's response is one of true repentance: "Look, Lord! Here and now I give half of my possessions to the poor, and if I have cheated anybody out of anything, I will pay back four times the amount" (19.8). Jesus responds, "Today, salvation has come to this house" (19.9). For Luke, encountering Jesus is personal, powerful, and in some sense divisive, as it forces a person to make a decision concerning this powerful teacher.

Luke: The Egalitarian Gospel

Luke is unusual among the Gospels not only in his highlighting of the female disciples who are traveling with Jesus but also in his positive portrayal of women throughout both the Gospel and Acts. One need only read the extensive birth narratives of both John the Baptist and Jesus to see that they are written from a female perspective.[3] In addition, through-out Luke's narrative, Luke often pairs stories of both men and women who prophesy, are healed, or serve as illustrations for Jesus's teaching.

At the very start of the Gospel, both Zachariah and Mary, the mother of Jesus, are contrasted in their response to the angelic message from God. Both Anna and Simeon prophesy over Jesus in the temple during his cir-cumcision in Luke 2.25–38. On separate Sabbaths, only a few verses apart in the narrative, Jesus uses the healing of a woman who has been unable to stand erect for eighteen years and a man suffering from Edema to teach his opponents the value of compassion above legal observance (13.10–17; 14.1–6). In Luke 15, when Jesus tells three stories that illustrate the value of the lost—the lost sheep, the lost coin, and the lost (prodigal) son—it is the story of the lost coin that catches our attention because the main character is a woman. What is striking about this parable is that God is portrayed as a woman, who seeks out the valuable lost.[4]

Luke is also unique among the Gospels in his early introduction of the female disciples of Jesus. Both Matthew and Mark reserve the intro-duction of the women followers of Jesus to the passion narrative since they are key witnesses to the death, burial, and resurrection of Jesus. Luke introduces the women disciples early in 8.1–3, along with the Twelve, as part of an entourage that regularly travels with Jesus. He names three of the more prominent female disciples, likely because they were well known in the early church, but then says that there were "many others" who helped to support Jesus and his followers from their own possessions. Although these women are not referenced again until the crucifixion, Luke makes clear that they are the same ones who had joined Jesus on the journey from Galilee to Jerusalem (23.49). They also serve as the eyewitnesses of the burial (23.55) and resurrection of Jesus (24.1–10).

The narrative of the "sinful woman," who washed and anointed the feet of Jesus in the home of Simon the Pharisee, is a story unique to the Gospel of Luke (Lk 7.36–39).[5] While we cannot know for sure what Luke has in mind, it is curious from a literary point of view that this encounter occurs just before the introduction of the female disciples of Jesus in 8.1–3 and lends credence to the assertion that this encounter with Jesus in Simon's house should be placed among the calls to discipleship in Luke. One might further suggest that this story is the counterpart to Peter's encounter with Jesus in Chapter Five. Both Peter and the woman are dreadfully aware of their sinful state, and both find themselves repenting at the feet of Jesus.

In fact, Luke Chapter Five consists primarily of discipleship encounters—first, Peter, James, and John (and perhaps others as well, possibly Andrew)[6] followed later by the story of Levi, who is called from his tax booth (5.27–32). In Chapter Six, Jesus chooses the twelve and preaches to them a basic sermon on kingdom values. By the end of Chapter Seven, we have the story of the sinful woman and the reiteration, at the beginning of Chapter Eight, that the Twelve along with many women are traveling with Jesus. In Chapter Nine the Twelve are sent out on a mission just before Jesus begins his journey to Jerusalem and the cross (9.51). It is almost as if these two encounters, one by a male disciple of Jesus and the other by a female disciple, bookend this section of the Gospel devoted to the Galilean ministry of Jesus.

The events in Simon's house also serve as a didactic moment, not only for Jesus, but also for Luke, who uses the story to advance his own themes. The contrast between the response to Jesus of Simon and the "sinful woman" is part of that dichotomy already discussed, which runs through the Lukan narrative. Not only is there the side-by-side contrast and comparison of male and female characters, so common in Luke, but also the ever-present contrast of response to Jesus's presence, which demands either belief or rejection. Jesus certainly takes opportunity in the narrative to draw upon their differing responses to him by making it a teachable moment. Simon has failed to recognize in whose presence he dines and, in addition, his own need of what his guest has to offer. The woman has not and she goes away forgiven.

Jesus's Identity

For Luke, this story advances another important theme—the lingering question of Jesus's identity, which is so prevalent in Luke Chapters Four through Nine. The narrator of the story gives us a glimpse into Simon's private thoughts as Simon questions whether Jesus is a prophet at all, since he tolerates the touch of this "sinful woman," which he certainly would not do if he really knew who she was (7.39). This contrasts with the crowd in Nain, which just a few verses earlier in the narrative had declared concerning Jesus, "A great prophet has appeared among us" (7.16). Simon now calls that very identity into question.

One might note, in fact, that much of Chapter Seven is devoted to issues of identity. The intervening story between that of Jesus's miracle in Nain and dinner at Simon's house once again questions Jesus's identity. This time it is John the Baptist who sends two of his disciples to ask, "Are you the one who is to come or should we expect someone else?" (7.20). Jesus's proof of identity is his own miraculous ministry. "Go back and report to John what you have seen and heard: The blind receive sight, the lame walk, those who have leprosy are cleansed, the deaf hear, the dead are raised, and the good news is proclaimed to the poor. Blessed is anyone who does not stumble on account of me." (7.22; cf. 4.18–19). In response to their visit, Jesus offers a clarification of the identity of John the Baptist as a great prophet, yet "the one who is least in the Kingdom of God is greater than he" (7.28). In an aside, the narrator also tells us that "the Pharisees and the experts in the law rejected God's purpose for themselves, because they had not been baptized by John" (7.30)—a fact that Simon the Pharisee will illustrate in the following narrative.

At the crescendo of the debate over Jesus's identity, Jesus asks his disciples privately, "Who do the crowds say that I am?" His disciples respond with a chorus of answers that we have already heard through the voice of Herod (9.7–9): "some say John the Baptist; others say Elijah; and still others, that one of the prophets of long ago has come back to life" (9.19). Then, Jesus asks the most important and defining question to his disciples, "Who do you say I am?" (9:20). Peter supplies the answer that the narrative has been anticipating all along, "God's Messiah."

Peter's insightful revelation is quickly followed by a first prediction of Jesus's impending suffering and death, which is then followed by the revelation of a glorified Jesus on the Mount of Transfiguration to the inner three of his disciples Peter, James, and John. Jesus appears in heavenly glory discussing with Moses and Elijah what he would soon accomplish in Jerusalem. It is here, in this moment, that the Father declares, "This is my Son, whom I have chosen, listen to him!" (9:35).

The two declarations by the Father, first at Jesus's baptism and now at his transfiguration, form brackets for this section of the Gospel in which Jesus's identity is carefully teased out. This final dramatic revelation leaves no question in the reader's mind, and more importantly in the disciples' minds, that Jesus is not Elijah come back to life nor is he simply a great prophet, but he is indeed the Messiah, the Son of God. This revelation is important for the disciples as they will be the ones to continue the ministry of Jesus throughout the world. While only the inner three disciples share this experience with Jesus, it will be they that provide the anchor and leadership for the rest.

Following this great revelation on the Mount of Transfiguration, the travel narrative begins. As mentioned in the introductory chapter, Luke places most of Jesus's discipleship teaching within this portion of the Gospel, which extends from Luke 9.51 to 19.44. Within these chapters, Jesus outlines the requirements of discipleship both through his teaching and through illustrative encounters with discipleship candidates.

Luke does not want the significance of Jesus's journey to be lost on his audience, so his introduction of it marks a clear shift in the narrative. He marks this shift in two very important ways. One, he uses key terms along with repetition to gain the reader's attention and to provide emphasis on this part of the narrative. Two, he recounts in rapid succession three unconnected but related encounters with would-be disciples. As far as Luke's Gospel is concerned, Jesus's Galilean ministry has ended at this point, his identity as the Messiah and Son of God has been established, and now what lies before him is the Father's will—the cross. In order to grasp the literary value of what Luke is doing, we need to examine these two significant features that serve to set the travel narrative apart.

Jesus Sets His Face

In 9:51, Luke tells us that "when Jesus's time was approaching *to fulfill* his destiny, he turned his *face* with firm *resolve* to go up to Jerusalem." I have paraphrased the verse based on the Greek expressions and have highlighted three key terms that need further exploration. Sometimes the full sense of what Luke is saying about Jesus does not always come through in English translations, so it is worth taking a moment to tease out a few of the nuances.

First, Luke uses the term *sumplērusthai* (συμπληροῦσθαι), which carries the sense of "fulfillment." Here, it is the idea that the time has arrived for Jesus to go up to Jerusalem to *fulfill* his purpose. I highlight this term because of its potential connection to Luke's preface (1.1), where the term *plērophoreō* (πληροφορέω) is used, which also carries the meaning of "fulfillment." Both of these terms are cognates of the same Greek word *plēroō* (πληρόω), which similarly means "to fulfill."

The importance of noting these connections is that Luke is continuing the theme he initiated at the beginning of his Gospel, which is to show how God is fulfilling in Jesus the promises he made through the prophets. The culmination of this theme will arrive in Lk 24.44 where Jesus tells his disciples, "Everything must be *fulfilled* that is written about me in the Law of Moses, the Prophets and the Psalms" (emphasis mine). Here Luke uses *plēroō* (πληρόω) to continue this theme.

Second, Luke uses the term *estērisen* (ἐστήρισεν), which expresses Jesus's attitude toward his goal in Jerusalem. This term captures the idea that Jesus has resolved to accomplish his purpose and nothing will keep him from it. He has made a resolute decision. This is an expression that can also be found in the Old Testament where one finds the phrase "to set one's face" (e.g., Ezek 6.2; 13.17; 14.8; 15.7; Jer 21.10). We have a similar idea in English in the idiom "to set one's jaw."[7] This metaphor paints the image of one's lower jaw set forward, teeth clinched, and jaw muscles tight. Such an idiom expresses that one is resolved and will not be dissuaded. This is Jesus's attitude toward his purpose and the Father's will.

Finally in 9.51, Luke uses the word *prosōpon* (πρόσωπον), which means "face," and he uses it two more times in each of the following verses, 9.52–53. The full idea being expressed in 9.51 is that Jesus "set his face toward Jerusalem." Again, this is an expression of determined purpose. The reiteration of the term "face" three times in these three verses only strengthens what Luke wishes to communicate to his readers. Not only is there a major shift taking place in the narrative and in the life and ministry of Jesus, but through the use of key terms and expressions, Luke lets us know the resolve with which Jesus viewed his mission that he would accomplish in Jerusalem. This resolve sets the tenor of the narrative to follow as Jesus will tell his followers, "And whoever does not carry their cross and follow me cannot be my disciple" (14.27, cf. 9.23). The tenor of the narrative is the tenor of discipleship.

The Three Would-Be Disciples

The three encounters with the "would-be" disciples, which follow beginning in 9.57, are somewhat unique to the Gospel of Luke both in their presentation and context.[8] The fact that there are three of them is suggestive of their importance to the narrative. Numbers in general are often symbolic in the Scriptures, and that is likely the case here. The number seven, for example, represents the number of completion, twelve the number of God's people, and three the number most often associated with the Godhead. For example, Moses sprinkles the anointing oil seven times on the altar and all its furnishings when he consecrates the tabernacle (Lev 8.11), and the Israelites marched around Jericho for seven days and seven times on the seventh day (Josh 6.3–4). In the New Testament, Revelation is the clearest example of the symbolic use of numbers, and there are other examples.

For Luke, the number three appears in significant ways in the Luke-Acts narrative to demonstrate the importance of a particular event to Luke's literary purpose. For example, the story of Peter and Cornelius and God's message to Peter of gentile acceptance is told three times in Acts (10.9–48; 11.1–18; 15.7–11, 14). Paul's Damascus road encounter with Jesus is recounted three times throughout Acts (9.1–19; 22.3–16; 26.9–18). Both of these events are of vital importance to Acts because they serve to establish the legitimacy of the gentile mission, a major concern of Luke's. The Holy Spirit also tells Paul three times in Acts that he will face arrest and persecution in Jerusalem on his final missionary journey, and, in Luke, Jesus predicts his own arrest, death, and resurrection three times. These are just a few examples, but as one can see, the thrice repetition of events is used to emphasize their importance.

These three encounters with would-be disciples, then, establish the travel narrative with a focus on discipleship. Just before these encounters, Luke has affirmed Jesus's own resolve to accomplish the Father's will through the thrice repeated use of the word "face." Jesus has "set his face toward Jerusalem." The question now arises in the narrative as to the resolve of those who would join Jesus on the way.

The first encounter begins in 9.57, where Luke writes, "As they were walking along the road, [someone] said to him, 'I will follow you wherever you go.'" In the beginning of this verse, Luke picks up the same Greek verb he used in 9.51, *poruomai* (πορεύομαι), which means "to journey," to announce Jesus's journey to Jerusalem. Therefore, in 9.57, the opening phrase could be translated, "As they journeyed on the way." Here, the verb is likely repeated to remind us of that journey just announced six verses earlier and Jesus's resolve to fulfill it. It is in this context that the first discipleship encounter occurs.

The first would-be disciple is a volunteer who approaches Jesus and announces her[9] intentions to follow him. Notice that she doesn't just say, "I will follow you," but says, "I will follow you *wherever you go*" (italics mine). The statement begs the question if this would-be disciple actually understands *where Jesus is going*. Does she think this son of David is heading to Jerusalem to claim his kingdom, or does she actually understand that Jesus is heading to Jerusalem to face rejection and the cross? After all, Jesus has told his twelve disciples privately what is about to happen to him (9.22; 44) and that if they want to be his disciple, they "must deny themselves and take up their cross daily and follow [him]" (9.23); but he has not told the crowds this, yet. He will tell them in 14.27, but as of now we the readers are the only ones privy to this information.

Perhaps this explains Jesus's response to this volunteer. Jesus tells her, "Foxes have dens and birds have nests, but the Son of Man has no place to lay his head" (9.58). This statement is even more impressionable since it follows closely on the heels of a Samaritan village's refusal of hospitality to Jesus (9.52–53), because the Samaritans saw he was journeying up to Jerusalem. Rejection is part of Jesus's journey and of those who join him on the way. Encountering Jesus always forces a decision, and some will follow while others reject him. Jesus's disciples will suffer the same plight, and Jesus wants this eager volunteer to count the cost before she makes the commitment to follow him "wherever [he] goes."

We are not told if this would-be disciple actually follows through with the commitment. This is an interesting and unusual aspect of this and the next two encounters. Perhaps Luke leaves us with open-ended encounters precisely so we might pause and wonder and in turn wrestle with the implications for our own discipleship. In fact, maybe that is why these three encounters with Jesus are so "raw," in that they give us no story context or names for these would-be followers as we have seen in other places in the Gospel. These characters simply appear and disappear on the scene, but each elicits a differing response from Jesus. Each of Jesus's responses reveals an aspect of discipleship with which every would-be disciple must wrestle.

The second and third encounters appear to be in parallel, as each would-be disciple responds to an invitation to follow Jesus, and each requests a deferment in order to "first" carry out familial obligations.[10] "Lord, first let me go and bury my father" (9.59), or "first let me go back and say good-by to my family" (9.61). Family obligations in this very community-oriented culture are important, and proper Torah observance demanded that one honor their father and mother. However, Jesus had already begun to outline the radical nature of kingdom demands in his own action and teaching. In 8.21, when Jesus is told that his own mother and brothers were waiting outside to see him, he told the crowd, "My mother and brothers are those who hear God's word and put it into practice."

With regard to discipleship, in 14.26, Jesus turns and tells the crowd following him, "If anyone comes to me and does not hate father and mother, wife and children, brothers and sisters—yes, even their own life—such a person cannot be my disciple." Jesus's teaching on the kingdom radically redefines social values and relationships, and, at first, his words to these two would-be disciples seem harsh and insensitive: "Let the dead bury their own dead" (9.60), or "No one who puts a hand to the plow and looks back is fit for service in the kingdom of God" (9.62). However, the issue here is not familial responsibilities, which Jesus understands and does not wish to undermine. The real matter is the demands of the kingdom and the true priorities of these would-be disciples. Are they concerned about the welfare of their families or simply not prepared to meet the obligations of true discipleship?

Responding to the Encounter

This threefold encounter at the beginning of the travel narrative prepares us for the explication of discipleship that follows. The open-ended nature of the encounters leaves the reader in thoughtful contemplation. What was their response to Jesus? Did they follow him and relinquish their own concerns? Or, did they walk away unwilling to acquiesce to the demands of discipleship? For many in the contemporary church (particularly in the United States), the assumption about salvation is that it is a private experience frequently made upon the appeal of a motivated preacher and has little ramifications for our day-to-day lives, beyond perhaps demanding regular church attendance and a new Bible reading program. Surely Jesus's call cannot be any more radical than this! This kind of discipleship is what Dietrich Bonhoeffer refers to as "cheap grace"[11]—discipleship without demands. At some point, when each of us has an encounter with Jesus, we must also answer the question, are we prepared to consent to the demands of discipleship?

What is clear in the Gospel of Luke is that while Jesus gained much notoriety and large crowds gathered around him, he was not trying to develop any political clout or gain in popularity polls. His teaching and actions are consistent and radically counter-cultural. He ate and drank with those many considered unworthy in a society where social status determined table fellowship. He spent time with those the religious elite considered unworthy for the kingdom of God and declared the kingdom is actually for them. He turned no one away, neither rich nor poor, socially connected or socially despised. Yet, his call to discipleship carries the same demands for everyone—you must deny yourself; take up your cross daily and follow me.

Luke seems to understand this "all or nothing" mentality of discipleship as he portrays it in subtle and not-so-subtle ways. A closer look at the encounter of Peter, James, and John with Jesus in Luke Chapter Five reveals some of the subtleties of the Gospel. When Jesus said to them, "Don't be afraid; from now on you will fish for people" (5.10b), Luke writes, "So they pulled their boats up on shore, *left everything* and followed him" (5.11). I emphasize the phrase, "left everything," because of its importance to revealing the nature of discipleship but also to revealing something about Luke's own perspective.

As we have already mentioned, the call of Peter, James, and John is found in the other Gospels, and Jesus's words of invitation to them to follow him are also nearly the same in Matthew and Mark. The difference is that Luke's Gospel is the only one to add that they "left everything." What is also interesting, and reveals that this addition is not just a unique happenstance for Luke, is that this exact same phrase is found a few verses later following the call of the tax collector, Levi. In the same manner, Luke writes, "Levi got up, *left everything*, and followed him" (5.27). This subtle addition reflects in part the fuller understanding that Luke has garnered through his own observation and experience of discipleship. What it means to "leave everything" we will explore in the next chapter.

1   Eugene H. Peterson, *A Long Obedience in the Same Direction: Discipleship in an Instant Society* (Downers Grove: InterVarsity, 1980), 13.

2   That is, the Sea of Galilee. Luke, unlike the other Synoptic Gospels, does not refer to this freshwater lake in Galilee as a "sea." In this matter, he is correct and more historically accurate. The other Gospels may call it a "sea" recalling the prophecy in Isa 9.1. I'm indebted to Dr. Steve Notley for this insight.

3   See the discussion in Richard Bauckham, *Gospel Women: Studies in the Named Women in the Gospels* (Grand Rapids: Eerdmans, 2002), 47–76.

4   I'm indebted to my colleague, Dr. Amy Anderson, for this observation.

5   There have been attempts to harmonize this story with the story of the anointing of Jesus by an anonymous woman in the home of Simon the Leper found in Mt 26.6–13, Mk 14.3–9, and Jn 12.1–8. In John's account, Jesus is anointed by Mary the sister of Martha and Lazarus. These anointing stories in the other three Gospels take place at a different place and time in the life and ministry of Jesus than that of Luke's Gospel. The stories outside of Luke all take place late in Jesus's ministry as a prelude to his death.

6   Compare Mt 4.18–22, Mk 1.16–20, and Jn 1.40–42.

7   Frederick William Danker, "στηρίζω," *BDAG* 945.

8   Matt 8.19–22 does contain a somewhat similar passage but with only two would-be disciples.

9   The Greek term in the text does not demand that this person be male or female, so it is conceivable that this could be a woman; however, the next two encounters seem to be men, based on the masculine pronouns used.

10   Joel Green, "The Gospel of Luke," *NICNT* (Grand Rapids: Eerdmans, 1997), 407.

11   Dietrich Bonhoeffer, *The Cost of Discipleship* (rev. 2nd ed.; trans. Kaiser VerlagMünchen; R. H. Fuller; rev. Irmgard Booth; New York: MacMillan, 1963), 61–86.

CHAPTER TWO

YOU CANNOT BE MY DISCIPLE

I was recently watching a sporting event on television when an advertisement for a popular soft drink was aired. The ad featured a young woman dressed in jeans and a green fatigue jacket worn loosely over a white T-shirt, on the front of which was a partially visible multicolored rainbow. As the young woman walked toward the camera holding an equally colorful can of this liquid ambrosia, she was warmly and gently talking to the audience, and her words were summed up in this one catch phrase, "just do you!"

The subtle and not-so-subtle message of the commercial sums up the current attitude of our postmodern culture. At least in the United States, individualism and personal rights are paramount, which results from our founding heritage. This two-pronged emphasis has led us in many directions, has become the basis of many of our laws, and has been a magnetic influence on our moral compass. The motto "just do you" and the rainbow emblem brandished in this commercial are verbal and nonverbal expressions of a plea for acceptance of individuals or groups, who express themselves in ways that others may find ideologically unacceptable or morally reprehensible. The mantra of the day is "tolerance."

It is not my intention here to impugn the idea of tolerance. As I stated in the previous chapter, Jesus welcomed everyone into his presence, and the church should do the same. There is, however, another side to this proverbial coin. I also stated that Jesus's call to discipleship carried the same demands for everyone—we must deny ourselves and take up our cross daily and follow him. Denying one's self and "just do you" sound like they go together about as well as oil and water. This, of course, has been the challenge for the church in every culture and every century, including the first, and that is resisting cultural influences that are contrary to its sacred teachings.

Even in the New Testament, such struggles are evident, particularly in the epistles of Paul. From his teaching on head coverings in the Corinthian church (1 Cor 11.2–16) to the wearing of jewelry in the Pastorals[1] (1 Tim 2.9–10), culture and religion have existed uncomfortably side by side. The Gospels reflect this struggle as well. Even the Jews, who wrestled long and hard to stay separate from the intruding Greco-Roman culture of the first century, were not immune to the inroads of cultural norms and ideology.

It is partly due to these societal influences that Jesus taught to his followers what we often call a counter-cultural Gospel. This is why he told parables about inviting the poor, the blind, and the lame to your house for a meal rather than your friends who could repay you, because he lived in a society where such favors were social currency. We call Jesus's kingdom message counter-cultural because then, and now, his teachings challenge social norms.

The motto, "just do you," expresses succinctly the postmodern stance of today. Adherents to postmodernism shun metanarratives—that is, that we all share the same story that defines who we are and what we believe. This, of course, is the very thing the Bible tells us—we do all have the same story and must come to believe in our one creator. Postmodernists also do not accept any objective standard by which one must be judged or by which one must live. Therefore, the only determinate for action and for morality is one's self. However, the boundary line is drawn when one's actions infringe on the rights of another. That is, as long as what I do doesn't hurt another, then it is acceptable behavior.

When I was in college, I worked with a ministry group that did evangelism on one of the local public university campuses. We would pair up and go into the dormitories and knock on doors engaging students in conversations about faith and ultimately would share the gospel message with them. I remember one particular evening after sharing the gospel with a young man that he made this statement to me, "If what I do doesn't hurt anyone else, then it isn't wrong." He made this remark in particular reference to the fact that he was sleeping with his girlfriend, which he couldn't see was hurting anyone.

To be honest with you, I don't really remember how we got on to that subject, but the conversation arrived at this moment in which he was trying to justify himself. At first, his statement actually kind of stumped me, because it seemed like a challenging one to refute. I don't remember what I ultimately said to him that evening, but I remember thinking later what the Apostle Paul said to the Corinthian men, who were visiting prostitutes and thought it not incongruous with their Christianity. "Flee from sexual immorality;" Paul writes, "All other sins a person commits are outside the body, but whoever sins sexually, sins against their own body" (1 Cor 6.18). He goes on to tell them that their bodies are the temples of the Holy Spirit and they should treat them as such. Sin injures the perpetrator, and that is ultimately God's concern.

This young coed's statement reveals the deception that is at the heart of sin. We are not the ones who determine the standard by which we live, nor are we the judges of right and wrong. When Adam and Eve made the decision not to take God at his word and to pursue the knowledge of good and evil on their own, they traded a life lived by God's wisdom for a life of foolish self-determination—"just do you."

Naturally then, the gospel message does seem to be and is counter-cultural because Jesus says, "deny yourself." Jesus taught that the standard one lives by is God's standard and that self-determination is self-destruction. "For whoever wants to save their life will lose it, but whoever loses their life for me will save it" (Lk 9.24). Contrary to postmodernism, we all do have the same story (metanarrative), and that is we "have all sinned and fall short of the glory of God" (Rom 3.23). The only way forward is to embrace the counter-cultural message of the kingdom. This is the first step on the journey of discipleship.

Discipleship Isn't for Everyone

On two occasions in the Gospel of Luke, Jesus speaks directly to his followers about the demands of discipleship. On the first occasion, Jesus has been praying in private (9.21–27) when he turns to his disciples and asks them who the crowds are saying that he is. The disciples respond with a variety of answers, but the climactic moment is Peter's pinnacle confession of Jesus as the Messiah (9.20). On the heels of this confession, Jesus "strictly warns them" not to tell anyone and makes the first of three predictions of his coming suffering, death, and resurrection (9.21–22). In the context of his own suffering, he outlines for his disciples the stark demands of discipleship (9.23–27)—"whoever wants to be my disciple must deny themselves and take up their cross daily and follow me" (9.23).

On the second occasion in Chapter Fourteen, Luke says that "large crowds were *traveling with him*." I highlight the phrase "traveling with him" in order to bring to mind, as Luke is likely doing as well, that we are in the travel narrative of Luke's Gospel. Recall that one of the chief topics of Jesus's teaching in the travel narrative is discipleship. For those who have joined him on the way, Jesus outlines more extensively and, in no uncertain terms, the requirements of discipleship.

At the end of Chapter Fourteen, we are about halfway through the travel narrative and Jesus has accumulated a large number of followers. Many had joined Jesus on the way to Jerusalem for a variety of reasons. Some were perhaps looking for a healing, perhaps others a miraculous sign that would ultimately put to rest their questions about his identity, or perhaps some were convinced that he was heading to Jerusalem to take his rightful kingdom. It was time to remind them that he was heading to Jerusalem not to take up a throne, but to take up a cross. He would indeed be crowned, but with thorns, and he would receive the title of king, but only in mocking derision.

In Luke 14.23–35, Jesus makes a number of statements that underscore the commitment required of his followers but are also designed to thin a crowd already too large. It isn't that Jesus doesn't want followers, but he wants fully committed followers, who understand the expectations of discipleship. Already we have examined the three would-be disciples he encounters at the beginning of his journey, each of whom had reasons not to join him on the way. His verdict, "No one who puts a hand to the plow and looks back is fit for service in the kingdom of God" (9.62). In 13.22–23, as Jesus was traveling from village to village on his way up to Jerusalem, someone asked him, "Lord, are only a few people going to be saved?" Jesus responded by saying, "Make every effort to enter through the narrow door, because many, I tell you, will try to enter and will not be able to" (13.24). The way is available to all, but not everyone is willing to meet the conditions.

The rich ruler, who approaches Jesus in Lk 18.18–30, is an example of one who was not willing. He came to Jesus and asked him what he must do to inherit eternal life. Jesus listed off the commandments by which he needed to live to keep God's first covenant. He proudly said that he had kept them from his youth. Then, Jesus said, "You still lack one thing. Sell everything you have and give to the poor, and you will have treasure in heaven. Then come, follow me." "When [the rich ruler] heard this," Luke writes, "he became very sad, because he was very wealthy." He wanted discipleship on his own terms.

You Must Hate (Really?!)

What then are the demands of discipleship? In Luke 14.25–35, Jesus issues three conditional statements, all of which, if the conditions are not met, end with the same consequence, you "cannot be my disciple" (14.26–27; 33 translation mine). The first two conditional statements appear in 14.26–27, have tremendous shock value, and were likely intended for this purpose. Jesus's teaching often contains hyperbole, and this section is no different.

He first tells the crowd that they must "hate father and mother, wife and children, brothers and sisters—yes, even their own life" (14.26) in order to be his disciples. For people who live in a Western culture, it is difficult for us to imagine the impact this statement likely had on the crowd. Even with the cultural difference, the statement taken at face value in any culture is difficult to process.

In the culture of first-century Palestine, family and family obligations were paramount. We made some reference to this in the last chapter when discussing the would-be disciples of Chapter Nine, who used family obligations to delay their joining Jesus on the way. First-century Jewish culture was a culture of community and was also a shame and honor culture. This kind of culture is quite different from Western individualism, as the choices one makes are determined by the family and community to which one belongs. Successes or failures reflect honor or shame not just on the individual but on the family and community as a whole.

Even Torah obligations reflected this kind of community orientation. Property that was bought and sold in Israel had to be returned in the Year of Jubilee to the family, clan, or tribe to which it belonged, so that no one or no tribe would lose their inheritance in Israel. If a brother died and left a wife without children, it was the responsibility of the brother next in line to take his dead brother's wife and have children with her in order that his brother's name not be lost from the family. As one of the Ten Commandments, caring for parents was a prime obligation. In addition, marriage was to be kept sacred, and a newly married man was exempt from military service in order to spend time with his new bride. Given this cultural backdrop, one can understand why Jesus's statement here is so shocking.

For many interpreters of this passage, the first challenge is getting around the word "hate." Reverting to the original Greek isn't a lot of help as it carries a similar meaning as the English translation. Since this statement is incongruous with Jesus's earlier teaching to his disciples to "love your enemies, do good to those who hate you" (6.27), which happens to be the same Greek word for "hate" used here in 14.26, then Jesus must have something else in mind than the total disregard of one's family in favor of him.

As stated earlier, this is the language of hyperbole to capture the audience's attention and also to shock them into the reality of the demands of discipleship. Included in this statement is not only a "hatred" of one's family but of one's own life as well. Family hatred and self-hatred seem strong demands, but perhaps the second conditional statement of this passage, which follows in the next verse, will help to illuminate Jesus's demands: "and whoever does not carry their cross and follow me cannot be my disciple" (14.27).

Take Up Your Cross

In 9.23, Jesus had made a similar remark privately to his disciples concerning cross bearing. We spoke of this passage earlier where Jesus is praying in a private place when he asks his disciples who the crowds are saying that he is. Peter's confession of Jesus as Messiah is followed by Jesus's first passion prediction (9.21–22). Then, Jesus talks to his disciples about the parameters of discipleship: "Whoever wants to be my disciple must deny themselves and take up their cross daily and follow me. For whoever wants to save their life will lose it, but whoever loses their life for me will save it. What good is it for someone to gain the whole world, and yet lose or forfeit their very self?" (9.23–25).

In the next episode beginning in 9.28, which is linked to this private moment with his disciples (9.18–27) through a temporal marker, is the account of the transfiguration. In this moment, Jesus discusses with Moses and Elijah his "exodus" that he must accomplish in Jerusalem and concludes with the Father's declaration, "This is my Son, whom I have chosen, listen to him" (9.35). When Jesus and his inner three disciples come down from the mountain, they encounter a father whose son is in need of deliverance from demonic oppression. Jesus heals the boy, and, while the crowd is marveling at the miracle, Jesus turns to his disciples once again and predicts his death a second time (9.41). It is ten verses later that Jesus begins his ascent toward Jerusalem and the cross, that is, the travel narrative.

As we can see, the question of Jesus's identity has reached a climax in the Gospel. The revelation of who he really is, however, is a private revelation to only his disciples, yet at the same time the implications of his identity are also being revealed through his predictions of suffering. For the disciples, while they may believe that Jesus is the Jewish Messiah, they likely do not know what that really means. In their own minds, they may think that it means political revolution or, at least, that God will now restore Israel to its rightful place as the autonomous people of God. This is what they believed the prophets had told them and is certainly what most of their religious leaders expected.

Jesus will predict his passion a third time in 18.31–32 (cf. 22.37), at which point he will tell them that "everything that is written by the prophets about the Son of Man will be fulfilled." Here, Jesus affirms to them what will be later reinforced at the end of the Gospel that what is predicted in the prophets is that of a suffering Messiah (24.44). Luke tells us that his disciples did not understand what Jesus was talking about, because it was hidden from them (18.34). Even at his ascension, as recorded in Acts, they were still asking him about the restoration of Israel's kingdom (Acts 1.6). Of course, Jesus's disciples did come to understand all of this eventually, but it took time.

Following Peter's confession and Jesus's prediction of his own imminent suffering in Chapter Nine is Jesus's warning to his own disciples that the road on which they walk with him ends at a cross. In fact, if anyone wishes to be his disciple, they must take up that cross every day and follow him. The cross for Jesus is his singular purpose. It is the event toward which the Gospel is ultimately building. From Chapter Nine forward, the cross is continually in view, and the journey toward it looms persistently in the background. What Luke's Gospel clarifies is that the journey to the cross is the journey of discipleship.

While the journey for Jesus is quite tangible and the cross quite material, for the disciples the cross is a metaphor for the singular purpose and wholehearted commitment of following Jesus. The cross represents self-denial and the loss of one's life, which are really one in the same thing. All other concerns and cares of this world fade into the background as one commits to God's kingdom values. Luke understands this commitment to be a "daily" walk and not just a onetime event or mental ascent. Of the three Synoptic Gospel writers who record this statement of Jesus, Luke is the only one who has "daily" couched in the phrase (9.23).

Discipleship is a persistent walk of endurance. For Jesus, the cross is the reason he was born into the world, and it represents the Father's will for him. His oneness with the Father, indeed his love for the Father, demands that he fulfill that purpose. He lived his life with no attachments, "the Son of Man has no place to lay his head" (9.58); his family are those who hear the word of God and obey it (8.21); and he lived in total dependence on and obedience to God. He expected no less of his followers.

To take up the cross daily is to devote one's self to God's kingdom purpose with no regard to one's own comfort or worldly existence. To take up our cross daily means a devotion to the will and purpose of God in our lives above all else, because we were made to honor him. This is really what it means to "hate" one's family or one's life. It isn't the diabolical hatred that might first come to mind. That kind of hatred is self-centered and wishes harm to our neighbor. The "hatred" of which Jesus speaks reflects singular commitment to the purpose of God above all else that might pull at our attention. Jesus's use of hyperbolic "hatred" is intended to reinforce the opposite—self-sacrifice for the good of others. Elevating the Heavenly Father's will above all else, even our own lives, is to put others first, for that is a foundational principle of his kingdom. As Jesus told his disciples in the Sermon on the Plain, "Love your enemies… then you will be children of the Most High" (Lk 6.35).

The self-determination of Eden is, therefore, replaced with the self-denial of the kingdom. This is how we save our lives by living them for the purpose of the one who gave them. Self-determination means certain death, but self-denial means life. As Jesus told his disciples in John 10.10,

"I have come that they may have life, and have it to the full." Letting go and letting God guide our lives is the challenge of discipleship and the one thing that grates against our human nature. This is why it requires death to self.

The Cost of Discipleship

In Luke 14.28-32, Jesus provides two illustrations that drive home the point that everyone who desires to be his disciple needs carefully to count the cost. In the first illustration, he asks the crowd a rhetorical question about standard practice in undertaking a building project, "Won't you first sit down and estimate the cost to see if you have enough money to complete it?" The obvious answer is "yes," because everyone knows that budgeting is the most basic task before undertaking any costly project. So, also one must consider the cost of discipleship, for if we are unable to follow through with our commitment, then we bring shame on ourselves and on our Lord.

The second illustration follows on the heels of the first and is one that would also resonate with the crowd. This one is about a king who is considering going to war with another king. Jesus asks, "Won't he first sit down and consider whether he is able with ten thousand men to oppose the one coming against him with twenty thousand?" If he is not able, he will certainly sue for peace. Then follows the all-important third conditional sentence of this discipleship passage, "In the same way, those of you who do not renounce all of your possessions cannot be my disciple" (14.33).

Jesus speaks often about possessions to his disciples and would-be disciples in Luke's Gospel. Generally speaking, the rich, who have possessions, are not placed in a positive light, while the poor stand in the limelight. This latter phenomenon is a reflection of the kingdom reversal announced by Jesus in the Nazareth synagogue. This is the year of the Lord's favor, which means that the "first will be last and the last will be first" (13.30).

The relationship between disciples and their possessions will be considered in more detail in the next chapter, since it is a somewhat bewildering topic. However, it is suffice to say that this third conditional statement, along with the first two, equally emphasizes a disciple's singularity of purpose. Neither family relationships, personal interests, nor material possessions are important enough to keep us from the call to discipleship.

As is often the case with Jesus's teaching, Jesus drives home a singular point by illustrating it from a variety of perspectives. I have heard it said that if you want people to get a point, then you must repeat it at least a dozen times. I don't know if this is true or not, but as a teacher myself, I have learned that if you want people to get information, it must be communicated repeatedly and in a variety of ways.

For Jesus, he wants the crowd to understand that discipleship requires complete dedication to a purpose beyond themselves. Jesus might say, "Don't follow me for what you can get out of it, but for what you can give to it." The heart of the Father is one of generosity. He has given his only Son. Jesus's heart, too, beats in tandem with that of the Father, and Jesus gives his life. A disciple is called to no less than this kind of total commitment. "Deny yourself and take up your cross daily and follow me." Without this kind of total commitment, disciples lose their impact, their value, which Jesus calls their savor. So, Jesus concludes his teaching with an illustration of the salty commitment to discipleship.

The Salty Commitment to Discipleship

"Salt is good, but if it loses its saltiness, how can it be made salty again?" (14.34) is the final question that Jesus poses to the crowd. "It is fit neither for the soil nor for the manure pile; it is thrown out." Just like the contractor who builds a tower but can't finish, and a king who wages a war he can't win; salt that has lost its savor is of no value. A person who is not wholeheartedly committed to a cause will likely quit when the going gets tough.

Jesus knows that the path he is on, and on which he invites his disciples, is difficult. It is not for the faint of heart and requires commitment all the way to the end, even if the end is a cross. If the crowd had been shocked by Jesus's previous statements and were still puzzling over them, these three illustrations hopefully would bring his point home. The final and third metaphor of salt is one anyone of them would have understood.

Salt in the first century was a valuable commodity. Not only is it a preservative, but it makes food savory. It is said that the English word "salary" derives from the Latin for salt. "Salary" corresponds to the Latin word *salarium* which has at its root the word *sal*, which means "salt." *Salarium* referred to the allotment of money Roman soldiers were given so they could buy this precious commodity of salt. Thus, the expression often used today that someone is "worth their salt" derives from this ancient use of salt as a form of payment for service. The crowd following Jesus, then, would have immediately understood that salt that was no longer savory had lost its value and therefore rather than being a treasure would become trash. What makes salt valuable and which belongs to its very essence is its savor. Salt without savor is not salt. It is worthless.

The very essence of a disciple's heart is single-hearted devotion to the kingdom. It is possessions, and even relationships drawn out of perspective, that can distract a person from such devotion. Such distraction is illustrated by someone looking back while plowing, as Jesus told the would-be disciple of 9.62. Jesus told his disciples, "No one can serve two masters. Either you will hate the one and love the other, or you will be devoted to the one and despise the other. You cannot serve both God and [material wealth] (mammon)" (Lk16.13).

This single-hearted devotion is the savor of a disciple and if lost, makes the disciple of no value. Such disciples are lost to the kingdom and only bring embarrassment to themselves and their master, because they started and couldn't finish. Like the Parable of the Sower, only a small portion of the hearts that receive the Word actually bear fruit. Perhaps this is why, in Chapter Fourteen, Jesus cautions the crowd with the same final words he used at the end of the Parable of the Sower, "Whoever has ears to hear, let them hear."

1   The "Pastorals" is the collective name for 1 and 2 Timothy and Titus in the New Testament.

CHAPTER THREE

TREASURE IN HEAVEN

A s was mentioned briefly in the last chapter, how disciples handle their possessions is an important part of the discipleship journey. Luke's Gospel actually has much to say about wealth, possessions, the rich and poor, and their relationship to the kingdom of God. Much of the material on these subjects is presented through Jesus's teaching but also reverberates throughout the narrative stories, and most of it is unique to the Gospel of Luke. Its uniqueness does not imply that it is not important. On the contrary, the presence of this unique perspective demonstrates Luke's own interest in discipleship and provides us a treasure trove of Jesus's teaching on what it means to join Jesus on the way.

Jesus told both his disciples and the rich ruler to sell their possessions and give them to the poor and they would have treasure in heaven (12.33; 18.22). In 14.25–35, which was the primary focus of the last chapter, Jesus tells the crowd that unless they renounce all their possessions they cannot be his disciples. Just taking these three texts into consideration would leave the impression that a vow of poverty is required of every true disciple. Once the larger context of Luke-Acts is taken into consideration, however, we will find that this is not the intention behind these texts. Having possessions isn't wrong—it's our attitude toward them that makes the difference.

An understanding of the topic of wealth and possessions in Luke begins with a consideration of the contours of Jesus's ministry as presented in the Nazareth synagogue. The Nazareth story is a unique episode in the Gospel of Luke and sets the stage for the presentation of Jesus's ministry and teaching throughout the Gospel. It is not unique to Luke that Jesus visits Nazareth during his Galilean ministry, as this visit is recorded in the other Synoptic Gospels (Mt, Mark). What is unique to Luke are the details of the story and the placement of the narrative at the beginning of Jesus's ministry.

We are told that after Jesus's baptism and temptation in the wilderness, he returns "in the power of the Spirit" (4.14) to Galilee where he begins his itinerant ministry. Jesus's fame spread quickly across the region, and by the time he arrives in Nazareth, his reputation has preceded him (4.14–15). Jesus entered the Nazareth synagogue on the Sabbath and stood up to read Scripture. He was handed the scroll of Isaiah the prophet and read portions of two passages, Isaiah 61.1–2 and 58.6. After reading the texts, he sat down and began to speak.

The Year of Jubilee

Luke has strategically placed this episode in Nazareth at the beginning of Jesus's ministry as a sort of formal declaration of what Jesus's ministry will comprise. Luke will then tell story after story, in particular in the following four chapters, illustrating how Jesus is fulfilling these Isaianic texts. It is in fact this prophecy that sets the agenda for Jesus's ministry and in turn Luke's Gospel narrative.[1]

There are some key elements in this prophecy that deserve highlighting. The Isa 61.1–2 passage begins, "The Spirit of the Lord is on me because he has anointed me." The presence of the Holy Spirit in the life and ministry of Jesus will become evident through the miraculous power encounters in the Gospel. Luke is known for his unique emphasis on the power and presence of the Holy Spirit as the unseen force not only behind the ministry of Jesus but as the promise of the Father that fills and empowers the disciples in Acts (Lk 24.49; Acts 1.4–5). The time of God's favor has come, and his anointed Messiah has arrived. This is the message that Jesus is relaying to the hometown crowd.

The final phrase of the passage Jesus reads from Isaiah is the proclamation of the year of the Lord's favor (Isa 61.2), which is a metaphorical reference to the Year of Jubilee. In Mosaic Law, the Israelites were to observe every fifty years a Year of Jubilee, which was a year in which all property that had been sold was to be returned to the original owner, all Hebrew slaves were to be set free, all debts were to be cancelled, and the land was to rest from farming (Lev 25.8–13).

This year also marked a time of "remission" for the people and the land. It began with the Day of Atonement in the forty-ninth year, the remission of the peoples' sins by God, and concluded with the people's forgiveness of one another's debts. The land was returned to its rightful tribes, clans, and families and given a rest from agricultural activity. All of these actions are a reminder to the Israelites that the Lord, whom they serve, is a redeeming God and that the land and the people ultimately belong to him (Lev 25.23).

Unfortunately, the Israelites had a difficult time remaining faithful to the Lord, so it is challenging to know how often Jubilee was actually observed. What did happen in Judaism over time, however, is that the Year of Jubilee became a metaphor for God's ultimate deliverance of his people from sin and the oppression of their enemies.[2] This metaphorical thinking is what is on display in Isaiah 61.1–2 and is to what Jesus is alluding. Jesus is announcing that the long-awaited Jubilee has arrived and that he is in fact proclaiming its inauguration. He outlines the agenda for this metaphorical year as well as his ministry through this Isaianic passage—"to proclaim good news to the poor… to proclaim freedom for the prisoners and recovery of sight for the blind, to set the oppressed free."

The first item on this prophetic agenda is the proclamation of the good news to the poor. We noted earlier that the poor figure prominently in Luke as do their counterpart, the rich. In first-century Palestine, there were "the haves" and "the have nots," those who wielded power and the powerless. This situation is not unique to first-century Palestine but is characteristic of every culture down through the ages. As today, also in Jesus's day, money and power walk hand in hand. This fundamental relationship and cultural characteristic are what help make Jesus's message so universal and timeless.

Jesus came to institute the long-awaited Jubilee that would challenge cultural values and bring release to those long oppressed. This is why those in power, "the haves," were so threatened by him and sought to silence his voice. This is why they crucified him. Of course, little did they know that his crucifixion, his "exodus" that he must accomplish in Jerusalem, was in fact the Day of Atonement that inaugurated the Jubilee. As the Apostle Paul says concerning this mystery of God's purpose, "None of the rulers of this age understood it, for if they had, they would not have crucified the Lord of glory" (1 Cor 2.8).

The reversal inaugurated by Jubilee is seen early in the Gospel through several of the speeches made within the birth narratives. Mary's song declares, "He has brought down rulers from their thrones but has lifted up the humble. He has filled the hungry with good things but has sent the rich away empty" (1.52–53). Zechariah, John the Baptist's father, declares concerning the remission of sins, "And you, my child, will be called a prophet of the Most High; for you will go on before the Lord to prepare the way for him, to give his people the knowledge of salvation through the forgiveness of their sins" (1.76–77).

The good news that Jesus is to proclaim and that he announces to the poor is that the time of God's favor is here. Sins are being remitted and the oppressed are being set free. A careful look at Jesus's ministry in Luke demonstrates that he spends much of his time with the powerless of society. When he was criticized by the Pharisees and the Law teachers for eating with the wrong people, Jesus replied, "I have not come to call the righteous, but sinners to repentance" (5.32; cf. 15.1–2). Forgiveness of sins is part of the Jubilee and is Israel's greatest need. When Jesus is presented with a paralytic for healing, he says, "Friend, your sins are forgiven" (5.20). His point is, he tells the once again disgruntled Pharisees and law teachers, "I want you to know that the Son of Man has authority on earth to forgive sins" (5.24) and promptly heals the man.

The marginalized in Luke are represented through a variety of characters as Jesus passes through Galilee. As mentioned previously, women figure prominently in Luke and are often paired with men in the same or similar stories. Women are not power brokers in this patriarchal society, yet Jesus forgives their sins (7.48), delivers them from demon oppression (8.2), raises their dead son (7.14–15), and heals them from lifelong illnesses (13.10–13). He allows them to touch him (8.46–48), which risks ritual impurity, just as he touched and healed unclean lepers (5.13). He uses children to illustrate kingdom principles (9.47; 18.16–17), and sits at table with hated tax collectors, even calling at least one to be his disciple (5.27–28; 19.5).

Many of Jesus's encounters with both the rich and the poor take place at table. This is a prominent characteristic of the Gospel and serves as a model for the kingdom of God. In this community-oriented culture, table fellowship is very important and could often reflect social divisions. Jews, for example, refused to eat with Gentiles for purity reasons. The Jewish religious elite refused to eat with anyone whom they considered ritually suspect, even if they were fellow Jews. Those who didn't observe Torah according to their religious standards did not merit fellowship.

For the Greco-Roman culture at large, which also certainly influenced Judaism, one usually ate with their social equals. If one received an invitation from a person of higher social class, it would be bad form to refuse the invitation, as the invitation would be an honor bestowed and an offer up the social ladder. This is the cultural background to Jesus's parable of the banquet (Lk 14.16–24), in which a man prepares a banquet and then notifies his invited guests that everything is now ready. One by one they refuse his invitation with frivolous excuses. "I have just bought a field, and I must go and see it;" "I just got married, so I can't come." Their refusal angers the man who immediately sends his servants out into "the streets and alleys" to invite the "poor, the crippled, the blind, and the lame... so that my house will be full." The invitation previously given has been shamelessly refused, and since they did not find the invitation worthy of their time, he will invite those everyone would consider to be unworthy.

The parable, of course, is a judgment on the Jewish religious leaders, who have refused the invitation of the king of heaven to dine in his kingdom. Now, the invitation is extended to those they clearly feel are not worthy, but in fact are the ones for whom the Jubilee is designed: those who are oppressed, poor, and captive—the powerless. The table is an intimate place for friends and for family. Jesus was demonstrating to his followers and to his enemies that in the kingdom of God, everyone is equal and everyone is family. "My mother and brothers are those who hear God's word and put it into practice" (Lk 8.21).

Jesus's instruction, then, to the rich was not to invite their friends, relatives, or even rich neighbors to their home for a meal, but to "invite the poor, the crippled, the lame, the blind, and you will be blessed. Although they cannot repay you, you will be repaid at the resurrection of the righteous" (14.13–14). The implication of Jesus's teaching is that social barriers are removed in the kingdom of God. Jesus would eventually institute his own fellowship meal with his disciples that is forged out of the Passover meal, the exodus event, which he would share with his disciples in Jerusalem the night of his arrest. This meal, comprised of the bread of his body and "the cup of the new covenant in my blood" (Lk 22.20), is shared at a table of equality among the family of God.

The Proper Attitude Toward Possessions

The social barriers Jesus addressed were usually the result of a dramatic divide between the rich and the poor. Wealth brought with it power and prestige, and so became the preoccupation of many in Jesus's day, much like it is in contemporary culture. Wealth, riches, and possessions, also called "mammon" in Greek, occupy a noticeable place in Jesus's teachings as recorded in Luke. There are several key passages to consider when looking at Jesus's teaching on possessions and a disciple's attitude toward them.

The first is found in Luke 12.13–34 at which time a person in the crowd demands, "Teacher, tell my brother to divide the inheritance with me." Jesus responds, "Man, who appointed me a judge or an arbiter between you?", and then warns the crowd, "Watch and be on your guard against all greed, because a person's life does not consist of the abundance of their possessions" (translation mine). Immediately, Jesus tells a parable to the crowd designed to illustrate this warning followed by teaching to his disciples about true abundance.

The parable that Jesus tells the crowd is often entitled the "Parable of the Rich Fool" (12.16–21). This parable is one of several parables unique to the Gospel of Luke, which highlight Jesus's extensive teaching on worldly possessions. The parable is a simple story and one that would resonate with his agrarian audience. It's a story of a man who planted and harvested a bumper crop and didn't have sufficient space to store his abundant harvest. He, therefore, decided to tear down his storage barns and build larger ones in order to accommodate his newfound wealth. Finally, feeling secure in his great fortune, knowing he had plenty of grain stored up for several years to come, he relaxes and says to himself, "You have plenty of grain laid up for many years. Take life easy; eat, drink and be merry."

However, there is a major oversight in his plan; the security that he thinks he now enjoys is only a fleeting mirage, because he has invested himself in temporal wealth rather than in eternal riches. God comes to him and says, "You fool! This very night your life is being demanded of you. And the things you have prepared, whose will they be?" The moral of the parable: "So it is with those who store up treasures for themselves but are not rich toward God."

A comparable example from contemporary life might be an entrepreneur or an investor who has made some wise business choices that have resulted in a store of great wealth. This newfound wealth provides a measure of comfort for the moment and security for the future. In a similar manner, a faithful employee might squirrel away sums of money in a 401K in order to secure a lucrative and comfortable retirement.

It should be noted that Jesus doesn't condemn the accumulation of wealth. He says, "So it is with those who store up treasures for themselves *but are not rich toward God.*" If he had simply said, "So it is with those who store up treasures for themselves," then the moral of the parable would take on a different tone. The problem with the rich fool is that his foolishness comes from thinking worldly wealth is an end in itself.

The request from the man in the crowd opens an opportunity for Jesus to instruct his disciples on their attitude toward quotidian needs, such as the basic necessities of food and clothing (12.22–31). Luke tells us in 12.22 that Jesus is now speaking to his disciples rather than the larger crowd to which he had addressed the parable. There are several occasions in the travel narrative where Luke informs his readers that the teaching that Jesus is doing is directed toward his disciples (e.g., 12.1; 16.1; 17.1, 22; 18.1). It isn't that others aren't present or don't hear the teaching to his disciples (cf. 16.1, 14; 12.1, 41), but these narrative markers serve to highlight the focus on discipleship formation, as he travels toward Jerusalem.

The parable told to the larger crowd and the subsequent teaching addressed to the disciples are linked in the narrative by the word, "therefore," located in 12.22 in most English translations. The Greek text confirms this connection between the two sections with a somewhat idiomatic phrase which could be translated "for this reason."[3] Jesus's instructions to his disciples, then, have their foundation in the Parable of the Rich Fool and, in particular, the moral of the story that highlights the importance of being rich toward God.

In the parable, the farmer found solace in his bumper crop because he believed all the usual worries of life would be assuaged by his newfound wealth. The parable likely resonated with the crowd that followed Jesus, since financial survival was a daily concern. Many of the dirt farmers of Palestine were only one drought away from complete disaster. Knowing that there was plenty stored up as a hedge against life's unexpected downturns would have been appealing to them. However, through the parable Jesus redirects their attention away from such concerns and toward what is truly important—their pursuit of God. What would happen if your life were to end tonight? This is the question asked in the parable but is really the question being posed to the crowd and even to us. Have we invested our energy, time, and money in the correct pursuits in order to be certain that we will be welcomed into an eternal reward?

In the passage that follows the Parable of the Rich Fool, Jesus tells his disciples how they can have everything if their life's focus is placed on the proper values. Jesus uses a common Jewish technique of teaching called *qal va-homer*, which employs a lesser to greater style of argumentation. It is an *a fortiori* argument in which one assumes that if something is true of a lesser example, then it applies to the greater. He reasons with his disciples that if God feeds the birds, even though they neither sow nor reap, then how much more God will do the same for them. In like manner, if God clothes the grass of the field with its own unique beauty, which is here today and gone tomorrow, how much more will he clothe them. The implication for the disciples is that God greatly values them, and human beings in general, as the pinnacle of his creation. Therefore, he will see to their needs as they devote themselves to him.

Jesus is really calling the crowd and his disciples back to covenant relationship with Yahweh. God's blessings on his people for covenant faithfulness included ample provision for food, clothing, and general security (Ex 23.25–26; Deut 11.13–15; Deut 28.1–14). It is their sin that has separated them from God and removed his blessing. Jesus's command to the disciples, then, is "seek [God's] kingdom, and these things will be given to you as well" (12.31). Jesus assures his followers that God knows that they have need of these things. Their created purpose is not simply to pursue survival as the "pagans" do, but to pursue God's kingdom.

Lest Jesus's disciples mistakenly think that he has replaced one worry for another, he reassures them in 12.32, "Do not be afraid, little flock, for your Father has been pleased to give you the kingdom." These words are reminiscent of a passage found only in the Gospel of Matthew where Jesus says, "Come to me, all you who are weary and burdened, and I will give you rest. Take my yoke upon you.... For my yoke is easy and my burden is light" (11.28–30). Jesus has told his disciples not to pursue food and clothing (Lk 12.29) but to pursue God's kingdom (12.31).[4] The pursuit of worldly needs is burdensome and creates anxiety. The pursuit of God's kingdom does not.

In the final two verses of this passage, Jesus tells his disciples what they should do with the possessions they have. He says, "Sell your possessions and give to the poor. Provide purses for yourselves that will not wear out, a treasure in heaven that will never fail, where no thief comes near and no moth destroys. For where your treasure is, there your heart will be also" (12.33–34). As a follower of Christ, this has always been a challenging passage for me to understand. My first impression of the passage is that Jesus is asking his disciples to sell *everything* they have as part of their devotion to him. After all, in a passage we considered in the last chapter (14.33), Jesus tells the crowd unless they renounce all of their possessions, they cannot be his disciples. However, I know in the history of the church that vows of poverty or living a destitute itinerate life have not been the mainstream teaching of the church, nor has it been the practice of most believers. Of course, the Christian church in many ways through the centuries lost its way, and so using church history as an exemplar isn't so comforting.

Personally, in my own pursuit of God over forty plus years, God has never asked my wife and me to divest ourselves of everything we own as a condition of discipleship. However, I will say that God's call on our lives has required, at times, to live with want or even to sell what we have to accomplish his mission. In the mid-1990s, God called us to overseas missions, which eventually required us to sell nearly everything we owned. One Saturday morning as we waited for the start of our yard sale, I remember the sadness I felt as I saw my wife sitting alone in a chair on the driveway ready to sell the things that just a few years earlier had been our wedding gifts. My wife is a very sentimental person and these possessions were precious to her. Parting with them was a challenge for her, but she valued more highly God's call to mission. This is how a disciple views her possessions, and this is what Jesus is trying to teach his disciples. Having them isn't wrong, holding on to them is.

The Proper Perspective on Possessions

It should be noted, first, that the focus of Jesus's discipleship teaching is the proper perspective on worldly possessions, particularly life's daily needs. Survival is the pursuit of every human being and is the innate instinct of every living thing. So, we pursue money, or more broadly wealth, in order to secure our survival. It is very easy for life's cares to overwhelm us and for our focus to be consumed by the accumulation of things, which offers us a sense of security and well-being. Jesus's teaching to his disciples is that such focus is misguided and wealth doesn't provide security. Remember the Parable of the Rich Barn Builder. It is their heavenly Father who provides security as well as true wealth. Their attitude toward possessions is to hold them not as security but as a tool to serve the kingdom.

Jesus did not tell his disciples to sell *everything* they have, but to sell their possessions so that they might be able to give to the poor.[5] The poor in Luke are not just the financially destitute, but the poor are anyone who has been marginalized, victimized, or are otherwise powerless to gain justice for themselves. This category would include children, the sick, and infirmed but also could include tax collectors like Levi and Zacchaeus, who were both wealthy but marginalized by their own people. It is for these people that the kingdom of God is good news, because the time of God's favor has come. The kingdom of God brings justice and hope to those who have none.

Jesus's disciples are to live lives that mimic kingdom values. They are to use their possessions, even their very lives, to advance the kingdom, not just in word but in action. Since Jesus has proclaimed the year of God's favor, that is, Jubilee, then the principles of God's Jubilee must apply. Jubilee means the redistribution of property. One of the foundational principles behind Jubilee is that the land in which the Israelites lived did not belong to them but to God. This is the reason why they were not allowed to sell the land permanently but could only value land based on the number of crops it would yield before Jubilee, when the land would revert to the original owner (Lev 25.13–24). Israel's use of and existence in the land was based on their faithfulness to God's covenant. It was their lack of faithfulness that resulted in their expulsion from the land, at which time the land enjoyed the Sabbath rest it had been denied during their unfaithfulness.

Not only did the land belong to God, but so did the people (Lev 25.42). Therefore, when an Israelite became poor, they were to be helped, "so that they can continue to live among you" (Lev 25.35). If a poor person sold themselves in order to pay a debt, they were not to be treated as a slave but a hired worker and were to be released along with their children during Jubilee.

One can see, then, that Jesus is simply reiterating the principles of Jubilee in his own ministry. This is because the operative word for Jubilee is redemption. People are to be redeemed, and so is property. Jesus encourages his disciples to completely depend on their heavenly Father for their provision because they belong to him. So in the case of the first Israelites, as the disciples seek God's kingdom, God will provide for all of their needs (Lev 25.18–22). In turn, they are to care for those among them who can't care for themselves, since the possessions they have really belong to God and are distributed by him for the good of all. Since their heavenly Father is generous with them, they are to be generous with each other (Deut 15.7–11).

We see the Jerusalem church in Acts living out this principle when Luke writes, "All the believers were together and had everything in common. They sold property and possessions to give to anyone who had need," and "all the believers were one in heart and mind. No one claimed that any of their possessions was their own, but they shared everything they had" (2.44–45; 4.32; cf. 6.1). The purpose of such redistribution of wealth was for the good of the community, so that no one would be in need. We don't see this kind of communal sharing emphasized among any of the other churches mentioned in Acts; however, we do see Paul collecting an offering from his gentile churches in order to deliver it to the poor in Jerusalem (Acts 24.17). No doubt Luke wants his readers to know that the discipleship principles that Jesus laid out in the Gospel were lived out in Acts.

Possessions for a disciple of Jesus are not an end in themselves but a means to an end. Jesus restates this principle more clearly another time when addressing his disciples in Luke 16.1–13. In this passage, Luke records another unique parable known as the Parable of the Dishonest Manager. In this parable, Jesus tells the story of a manager, who is the financial overseer for his wealthy master. He is confronted by his master for suspected mismanagement of funds and is told to give an account of his books, because he is going to be fired.

The manager panics because he is about to lose his position and doesn't know how to do anything else—"I'm not strong enough to dig, and I'm ashamed to beg" (16.3). He devises a plan to make sure that he has friends who will take care of him after he loses his job. One by one he calls his master's debtors in and reduces their bills—one by half and another by twenty percent. When the master finds out what his manager has done, Jesus says the master commends the manager because of his shrewdness. Jesus draws the following moral from the parable: "For the people of this world are more shrewd in dealing with their own kind than are the people of the light. I tell you, use worldly wealth to gain friends for yourselves, so that when it is gone, you will be welcomed into eternal dwellings" (16.8–9). In this passage, Jesus clarifies how he views possessions. They are to be used to further the kingdom and thus provide eternal rather than temporal security.

The Proper Use of Possessions

There are passages in Luke from which one can glean a practical, if not subtle, understanding of how disciples might use their possessions for the sake of the kingdom. In Luke 8.1–3, Luke writes that, in addition to the Twelve that traveled with Jesus from town to town, there were also several female disciples who "were helping to support them out of their own means" (8.3b). The "them" in this passage refers to Jesus and his company of disciples, the women included.

We discussed in the last chapter that one of the conditions of discipleship announced to the crowd is the renunciation of "everything you have" (Lk 14.33). What is not readily apparent is the connection between 14.33 and 8.3. English translations generally don't divulge that the same Greek word is used in both passages, *huparchousin* (ὑπάρχουσιν), which in the NIV is translated, "everything you have" in 14.33 and "their own means" in 8.3, but in actuality simply means "possessions."

These two passages seem contradictory and beg the question, how does Jesus tell the crowd that renouncing possessions is a requirement of discipleship and at the same time derive his ministry support from disciples who have possessions?! Clearly, just having possessions is not wrong. Jesus is not calling for destitute disciples, but he warns them to avoid the false sense of security they provide and not to allow them to distract from kingdom priorities.

There is a second parable in Luke Chapter Sixteen that serves to drive home this point. Jesus tells the story of an unnamed rich man and a poor man named Lazarus.[6] This story, too, like the Parable of the Dishonest Manager, is unique to Luke's Gospel. The poor man, Lazarus, is placed every day to beg outside the rich man's gate, but the rich man fails to take pity on him or even to take notice of him. Eventually, both the rich man and Lazarus die, and the rich man is unceremoniously buried, while Lazarus is carried by the angels to Abraham's bosom.

In the afterlife, the tables are turned as the rich man is tormented, but Lazarus is comforted. The rich man begs for mercy, just a drop of water, because he is tormented in the fires of Hades. In the voice of Abraham, the justice of the scene is summed up, "Son, remember that in your lifetime you received your good things, while Lazarus received bad things, but now he is comforted here and you are in agony" (16.25).

The parable serves as a warning but also as summation of Jesus's teaching on possessions. Possessions are not an end in themselves, and those who think they are will be surprised in eternity. They will find that their investment in this life rather than the afterlife has left their account short.

Wealth is to be used to serve kingdom purposes that result in a storage of treasure in heaven, where true wealth lies and every heart should be turned.

Two final contrasting illustrations of a disciple's proper use of possessions are the stories of the rich ruler and the tax collector, Zacchaeus. Luke places these stories in close proximity to one another in the narrative and are, therefore, likely intended to offer opposing examples. In the last chapter, we touched briefly on the rich ruler, but a quick outline of the story here will suffice to recharge our memory.

In 18.18, Luke tells us that a ruler comes to Jesus and poses the following question, "What must I do to inherit eternal life?" Jesus lists off a number of commandments from the Decalogue, which he rightfully assumes the ruler should know. We are not told who this "ruler" is or what he does, but one might assume that he is a synagogue ruler,[7] or at least a leader among the Jewish people. After all, he is, from his own testimony, a strict law observer—"All these [commandments] I have kept since I was a boy" (18.21). Jesus replies to him, "You still lack one thing. Sell everything you have and give to the poor, and you will have treasure in heaven. Then come, follow me" (18.22). Luke writes that Jesus's response made the ruler "very sad," because he was "very wealthy."

The response of the ruler becomes a teaching moment for Jesus: "How hard it is for the rich to enter the kingdom of God! Indeed, it is easier for a camel to go through the eye of a needle than for someone who is rich to enter the kingdom of God" (18.24–25). Those around Jesus who are listening, including his disciples, are incredulous at this remark and ask, "Who then can be saved?" The question betrays a common misunderstanding of those who followed Jesus that wealth was considered a sign of God's blessing, while poverty, sickness, and general misfortune were seen as a curse from God for sinful living.

This is the reason for the Pharisees' and law teachers' indignation over Jesus's habit of spending time with "sinners" (5.30; 15.1). These "sinners" are the people living outside of the covenant and who are under God's disfavor. This ruler, however, is clearly a covenant keeper which must explain his wealth. He is living under the favor of God. This kind of logic helps explain the question, "Who then can be saved?!" Jesus holds out hope by reassuring those around him that "What is impossible with human beings is possible with God" (18.27 TNIV).

Peter, the most outspoken of the disciples, declares what is likely on everyone's mind—the proverbial elephant in the room; "We have left all we had to follow you!" (18.18). The disciples still don't fully grasp what it means to follow Jesus and in particular what role money, wealth, and possessions play in a disciple's life. In their favor, however, they have had an encounter with Jesus; they have been obedient to step out and join him on the way; and so such revelation will come through God, who is able to do the impossible.

It is not surprising, then, that Jesus pulls his disciples aside at this moment and reminds them what fate awaits him in Jerusalem (18.31–33). The cross is the Father's will for him, and, like he has taught them to do, he must take it up and accomplish that will. The first time Jesus spoke of his forthcoming suffering, death, burial, and resurrection was following Peter's great confession of him as the Messiah, and it was in that context he told them they too must take up their cross daily and follow him (9.23). This encounter with the rich ruler has set the stage for another reminder of what must be paramount in a disciple's life—the Father's will.

The second and last encounter we will discuss is that of Zacchaeus. Zacchaeus's story is an interesting one because it brings together a number of themes in Luke's Gospel in surprising ways, including the theme of discipleship and possessions. Throughout many of the Lukan passages, we have noted how the rich and the poor have been pitted against one another as polar opposites with the poor getting the better press. However, in Zacchaeus's case, he is not poor financially, yet he is considered one of the outcasts of his culture. Therefore, by definition, he would fit in the broad category of "poor" as defined by Luke.

Zacchaeus is a tax collector for the Romans, but he is also a Jew. Jewish tax collectors were despised by their own people, because they were not only stooges of the foreign oppressors, but also padded their own pockets by over-collecting taxes. The Roman authorities were aware of this practice and generally looked the other way. They didn't particularly care what was done by the collectors as long as the government got their share.

The story of Zacchaeus, like the "sinful woman" who washed Jesus's feet, is not typically considered a discipleship encounter in Luke. Jesus, for example, doesn't say to Zacchaeus, as he does to the rich ruler, "Follow me." However, like I argue for the sinful woman, I think that Zacchaeus's story belongs in the category of a discipleship encounter. First, he makes every effort to see Jesus, which includes climbing into a tree since he is of small stature. Second, Jesus singles Zacchaeus out for a personal encounter with him—"Hurry and come down, for I must stay at your house today" (19.5). Third, Zacchaeus is changed by the encounter, which is evidenced by a discipleship response—his handling of his possessions.

As mentioned above, Zacchaeus's story is set in contrast to that of the rich ruler. Zacchaeus, who is also wealthy, is by his own admission not a law observer. He has at least broken the commandment, "you shall not steal" (18.20), which the rich ruler had kept since he was a boy. Zacchaeus's encounter with Jesus does not result in him saddened but rather joyous as he declares, "Look, Lord! Here and now I give half of my possessions[8] to the poor, and if I have cheated anybody out of anything, I will pay back four times the amount" (19.8).

His possessions will not be an obstacle to following Jesus, as he does just what the rich ruler refused to do. Jesus's response to Zacchaeus is telling, "Today salvation has come to this house, because this man, too, is a son of Abraham. For the Son of Man came to seek and to save the lost" (19.9–10). Jesus had just declared in 18.24 that it is hard for the rich to enter the kingdom of God, yet God has done the "impossible" with Zacchaeus. A rich man has entered the kingdom of God!

The key to discipleship is surrendering ourselves and our possessions to God's will. This is what Jesus has been trying to tell his followers throughout this journey, as we saw in the last chapter, while discussing the three conditional statements of discipleship that we cannot be Jesus's disciple unless we deny ourselves (9.23), take up our cross, and follow him (14.23). Denial of self, "hating" one's family, and releasing our possessions (14.26, 33) can only be accomplished through the power of the Holy Spirit and is not learned overnight. Discipleship is a journey. Zacchaeus has heard Jesus's invitation and has chosen to join Jesus on the journey, which is evidenced by his obedience. Listening to the Master and responding to what he says is fundamental to discipleship and is the subject of the next chapter.

1   Luke does a similar literary technique when he records in Acts 2 Peter's quotation of the Joel 2.28–32 prophecy, which provides the paradigmatic verse for the Acts narrative and the ministry of the disciples.

2   For example, see 11QMelchizedek (11Q13) among the Dead Sea Scrolls.

3   This is the translation chosen by the *New American Standard Bible* 1995 update (La Habra, CA: The Lockman Foundation, 1995).

4   The same Greek verb for "pursue" is used in both verses.

5   The Greek word in the text means to give alms, but the implication is to help the poor.

6   Note how the rich man has no name but the poor man does. This only serves to heighten in a subtle way the favor that has now come to the poor.

7   Perhaps like Jairus, who is described as a synagogue ruler in Luke 8.41.

8   The Greek word for "possessions" used here is the same as the one discussed earlier in relation to Luke 8.3 and 14.33, *huparchontōn* (ὑπαρχόντων).

CHAPTER FOUR

WHY DO YOU CALL ME LORD?

"Did-you-hear-what-I-said?!!", the mom stated in staccato fashion to her little boy, in the middle of the Walmart aisle, right after he had done something she had just told him five minutes ago *not* to do. Of course, she may or may not have expected an answer from him, but her more than likely rhetorical question was, instead, an expression of frustration directed at his disobedience. Being a parent myself, I understand the sense of frustration that comes in these moments but also the loving discipline that often follows as we seek the best for our children.

Parents understand that listening, being obedient, respecting others, and honoring boundaries are important qualities to have in order to function in our communities. Jesus too recognizes that these are qualities vital to a disciple, who lives in God's community. In Luke 6.46, Jesus expresses perhaps a sense of godly frustration when he asks a similar question, "Why do you call me Lord, Lord, and do not do what I say?" This rhetorical question is the climactic moment to a teaching that had begun just a few verses earlier in 6.20, which outlines the qualities of Jesus's new covenant community.

A New Covenant

Jesus spent all night on a mountain in prayer and the next morning chose twelve disciples, whom he also designated apostles. He then came down with them from the mount and stood on a level place to teach. Reminiscent of Moses coming down from Mount Sinai, Jesus outlines the characteristics of those who live within the kingdom of God. His teaching is certainly counter-cultural, but not out of step with the principles God had set forth through Moses over a millennium earlier. Although Jesus establishes a new covenant through his death and resurrection, his ministry is a call to Israel and the nations to the principles of the first covenant.

The age-old problem with Israel was their lack of obedience, which had led to great suffering and exile from the land. God bemoans Israel's lack of heartfelt obedience through the prophet Isaiah when he says, "These people come near to me with their mouth and honor me with their lips, but their hearts are far from me" (29.13a). So God devised a new plan which he announced through the prophets, "'The days are coming,' declares the LORD, 'when I will make a new covenant with the people of Israel and with the people of Judah;'" and "'I will give them an undivided heart and put a new spirit in them; I will remove from them their heart of stone and give them a heart of flesh'" (Jer 31.31-34; Ezek 11.19-20; 36.26-28; cf. Heb 8.7-13). Jesus's new covenant community will be one that has experienced a transformation of the heart through a repentant encounter with him. Jesus tells the disciples, "Out of the good treasure of the heart a good person brings forth good fruit" (6.45 translation mine). Discipleship in the new community is expressed through heartfelt obedience that manifests itself in fruitful living.

Through disobedience, Israel had largely lost its identity as a people, having been scattered across most of the known world. Many had returned to the homeland but more had not. God in his great mercy had appointed a time that has now reached fulfillment in which he would restore the fortunes of Israel. It is in Jesus's coming that this new day has dawned and a new covenant community is being established (Isa 2.1-5).

In a symbolic act of his reestablishment of God's covenant people, before Jesus preaches his Sermon on the Plain (SOP),[1] he chooses twelve disciples who are symbolic of that community, a reconstituted Israel. This "new" Israel will not only be comprised of Jews but also Gentiles, as had been prophesied (Isa 42.6; 49.6).[2] This point is an important one for Luke who acknowledges the deep roots of the new covenant in what God is doing through Israel but also pushes hard the inclusion of the Gentiles, especially in his second volume, Acts (Luke 2.32; Acts 11.18; 13.46, 47; 14.27; 15.14; 28.28).

The Nature of the New Covenant Community

As a prelude to the SOP, Luke tells his audience that "a large crowd of [Jesus's] disciples and a great number of people" (6.17–18) from all the surrounding regions, including not only Jewish Palestine (Jerusalem and Judea) but also the gentile cities of Tyre and Sidon, "had come to hear him and to be healed of their diseases." There are three groups represented in this introduction—the twelve disciples whom Jesus had chosen; a larger crowd of disciples, presumably from whom he chose the twelve; and a very large crowd of people, from many of the surrounding regions. Even though there is a large and diverse crowd with Jesus, Luke tells us that Jesus's teaching is specifically directed toward his disciples (6.20).

The SOP is divided into three topical sections.[3] The first section (6.20–26) is a set of beatitudes and corresponding woes that reinforce the upside-down nature or reversal of the kingdom of God—"Blessed are you who are poor... Woe to you who are rich." Such reversal has already been characterized in the Gospel and will continue to be presented in Jesus's parables and teaching that follow. The first two beatitudes are placed in the present tense and the middle two in the future tense illustrating the already and not yet of the kingdom.

Jesus teaches his disciples here and elsewhere that they have to have the "long perspective," that is, they must think eschatologically. A disciple does not live for the moment but lives for the kingdom, which is both a present and a future reality. Some of what Jesus says has begun now in his ministry and will continue until it sees fulfillment in the eschaton, where God will meet out final justice. The parable of Lazarus and the Rich Man amply illustrates this eschatological reversal, where the rich man enjoys this life but suffers in the next, while Lazarus, who suffered in this life, dwells in the afterlife at peace in Abraham's bosom.

The beatitudes of the SOP correspond mildly to those in Matthew's Sermon on the Mount (SOM); however, there are more differences than similarities. Luke's beatitudes are very personal, as Jesus addresses them to his disciples in the second person with the larger crowd listening in. Jesus warns his disciples that the counter-cultural nature of his community will draw the ire of those who enjoy power and prestige in this life, and for that reason they must be ready for persecution that will surely follow. They are, however, to consider themselves blessed when they suffer because that will be a sign to them that they are indeed children of God. Israel's history is illustrative. The prophets that came from God were most often rejected by the people and persecuted or killed, as they challenged the sinful propensities of the community.

The second or middle section of the SOP (6.27–42) is marked by this opening line from Jesus, "to you who are listening I say," after which he addresses human relationships between those within and without the community. The main characteristic that Jesus commands is love expressed through generosity. Twice in this section Jesus tells his followers, "love your enemies" (6.27, 35). In addition, he tells them that they should "give to everyone who asks" and to "give, and it will be given to you" (6.38). How is one to love their enemies? Bless them, pray for them, offer them the other cheek, and "if someone takes your coat, do not withhold your shirt from them" (6.28–29). This attitude of practical generosity is what John the Baptist calls, "fruit in keeping with repentance" (3.8).

At the heart of this generosity is a concern for others. Jesus tells his disciples privately, later, that anyone who wants to be his disciple "must deny themselves" (9.23), as fundamental to following him. He will tell a crowd of followers essentially the same thing in Luke 14.26. Discipleship is marked by unconditional love of others that is generous and non-retaliatory. Retaliation results from a focus on self and an unwillingness to suffer wrong. Retaliation also springs from an unwillingness to forgive, which is why Jesus tells his disciples, "Forgive and you will be forgiven" (6.37). This generous love also extends to accepting the faults and failings of others.

The Pharisees and legal experts have been guilty of excluding others from covenant relationship with God based on their sectarian standard of judgment (11.37–52). Jesus is telling his disciples, as well as the crowd (which certainly includes Pharisees, Scribes, and Law experts), that retaliation and judgment belong to God. While helping one another to overcome personal weaknesses isn't excluded, Jesus admonishes them, "You hypocrite, first take the plank out of your eye, and then you will see clearly to remove the speck from your brother's eye" (6.42).

Thus, Jesus says "do not judge" and "do not condemn," rather "forgive" and "give, and it will be given unto you. A good measure, pressed down, shaken together and running over, will be poured into your lap. For with the measure you use, it will be measured to you" (6.37–38). The example and motivation for such generosity toward one another is their Heavenly Father, who will reward them for emulating his character, "because he is kind to the ungrateful and wicked." (6.35).

All of this, as mentioned above, has an eschatological or eternal perspective, as does most of Jesus's teaching on discipleship. Jesus tells his disciples to sell their possessions and give to the poor and they will have "treasure in heaven that will never fail" (12.33), and later he tells the rich ruler to sell all that he has and he will have "treasure in heaven" (18.22). To the disciples who have left everything he promises, "Truly I tell you, no one who has left home or wife or brothers or sisters or parents or children for the sake of the kingdom of God will fail to receive many times as much in this age, and in the age to come eternal life" (18.29–30). Disciples are living for the age to come, and every action taken in this life needs to reflect the values of that age, which has already begun in the ministry of Jesus.

Jesus's new covenant community, which he is establishing on earth, is a community that belongs to the age to come. So here, too, Jesus tells his disciples, and the crowd, that living by kingdom values results in a "great reward... in heaven" (6.23, 35). This is not to say that there is no reward in the present for indeed there is, as Luke 18.29–30 makes clear, but every disciple must maintain an eternal perspective. The Parable of the Rich Barn Builder (12.13–21) aptly demonstrates the danger of a myopic perspective.

The third and final section of the SOP is the climax of the sermon and is where the proverbial rubber meets the road. Even though Luke tells us that Jesus's teaching is directed to his disciples (6.20), one can't help but be aware that some, if not all, of Jesus's teaching is intended to be heard by the larger crowd and in particular the Pharisees, Scribes, and legal experts, who had come down from Jerusalem. The commands not to judge or condemn one another, and the command to get the wooden beam out of one's own eye before trying to remove the speck of sawdust from your neighbor's eye, certainly were aimed at the religiously arrogant.

Jesus warns that whom you choose to follow is the one you will emulate. "Can the blind lead the blind? Will they not both fall into a pit? The student is not above the teacher, but everyone who is fully trained will be like their teacher" (6.39–40). The religious leaders are blind guides, and Jesus tells his disciples that they can know this by the fruit that their leaders produce. The issue is, of course, listening and obeying. The religious leaders claim to follow God's law but in reality are living to please themselves—to keep power, line their pockets, and maintain their prestige. Following Jesus, of course, means emulating his character and obeying his teaching, so he ends the sermon with this rhetorical question, "Why do you call me, 'Lord, Lord' and do not do what I say?"

Commentators often wonder to whom this question is addressed.[4] Jesus has just chosen his twelve disciples, and there is little evidence that anyone at this point is calling him "Lord," in this authoritative sense. In fact, as we have noted before, looming over the first eight chapters of Luke is the overarching question of Jesus's identity. The question Jesus poses, as already stated, is rhetorical, but I think Jesus has two things in mind. First, standing in his presence are the religious leaders who represent Israel's attempt, at its best, to reconnect with Israel's God, YHWH, yet, in all of their effort, they are still far from him. Jesus asks the same question that has been asked through the prophets in a number of ways over the previous centuries. Second, Jesus is addressing a crowd of disciples and potential disciples, who must understand that listening to Jesus's teaching and obeying it are fundamental to following him. Luke understands this aspect of discipleship and begins here in this sermon to highlight it.

Hearing and Doing

This rhetorical question posed by Jesus inaugurates a theme in Luke that runs through the next few chapters, which we will call "authentic hearing."[5] Often implied in the Greek word meaning "to hear" is a sense of not only hearing what someone says but also responding with appropriate action. Much like the illustration used at the beginning of this chapter when a mother (or father) might ask, "Did you hear me?!", the implication is that, "you must not of because if you had you would have obeyed me."

Jesus's rhetorical question at the end of the SOP implies in perhaps a much gentler way the same thing, "Why do you call me, 'Lord, Lord' and do not do what I say." He then proceeds to give the crowd an illustration which paints a picture of the consequences that result when one "hears my words and puts them into practice," and when one does not. The illustration is a familiar one in which two builders each builds a house. The one who listens to Jesus's teaching is like a person who digs down to bedrock and lays the foundation of the house so that when the storms come, the house can withstand the flood. However, the one who "hears my words and does not put them into practice" builds the house on a poor foundation, and the house is destroyed during the subsequent flood.

Luke has set us up for this grand finale through subtle innuendos that begin in 6.18. He has told us that when Jesus comes down from the mount after choosing his disciples, "a great number of people… had come *to hear* him." After Jesus presents the beatitudes and the woes of 6.20–26, a shift in subject matter is noted through Jesus's remark, "To those who are *listening* I say." I highlight the two words in the previous quotes because they are the same Greek word. To make a play on the English words, the crowd has come *to hear*, but are they really *listening*? This will be the challenge that Jesus makes at the end of the sermon.

Whether they are listening will be determined by what they do, which will be evident in the fruit they bear. Jesus outlines the parameters of his new community, which are quite outside what the crowd likely expected. Most in the crowd probably came to see what they could get from Jesus, but he delivers a message about a community not built around self-interest but self-sacrifice. Listening to Jesus and doing what he says is at the heart of discipleship, which we will see as we continue to follow the "authentic hearing" motif through the next few chapters in Luke.

A Farmer Went Out to Sow

I love to garden. I mostly flower garden, but this past year, for the first time in many years, I decided to plant a vegetable garden. My love for gardening actually began with a vegetable garden I had when I was a kid. I remember when I was about twelve years old that I asked my parents if I could dig up a small corner of our backyard to plant some vegetables. They consented and so I was off. I don't really remember what I planted, but I do remember that it wasn't long before the garden was full of weeds—big tall weeds! I remember coming out one day and looking at it and thinking, "What a mess!" I also felt a little embarrassed, too, because the reason for the mess was my own neglect.

In all fairness, as a twelve-year-old kid, I didn't really understand all that went into cultivating and maintaining a garden. I did know this, though, pulling weeds was not my thing! I don't really remember if we got any vegetables from that small plot, but what the garden did accomplish is that it ignited a spark in my dad, who had been raised on a farm and had a latent love for growing things. Since we owned a large piece of property, the next year, my dad plowed up a plot of ground twenty times the size of my garden. He bought a garden tractor with all the attachments, and we had a garden to beat all gardens! Of course, guess who had to learn to pull weeds? That's right, me! I still don't like pulling weeds, but I learned if you cultivate the ground faithfully, then weeds don't get a chance to grow, and so, I have become a master with the hoe!

Gardening is probably one of the most universal activities. Every culture understands the principle of sowing and reaping. The agrarian culture of Jesus's day certainly did, and this is why Jesus so often used farming illustrations in his parables. The next location in the Gospel where the theme of authentic hearing is most visible is in Jesus's telling of the Parable of the Sower.

Once again in 8.4, Luke tells us that a large crowd from towns all around had gathered to Jesus, at which time, he tells them a parable about a farmer that went out into his field to sow his seed. The farmer sows his seed indiscriminately, which results in seed falling on a variety of soil types. Jesus highlights four soils—the hard trodden path, rocky hardened soil, thorny uncultivated soil, and good prepared soil. The seed on the hard trodden soil is an easy mark for hungry birds as the seed lay on the surface of the ground unable to penetrate. The seed on the rocky hardened soil and the thorny uncultivated soil is unable to reach maturity and so never produces good fruit. The fourth soil is the soil that is well cultivated and is ready to receive the seed, and so, the seed takes root and produces a crop one hundred times over.

The Parable of the Sower is found in all three Synoptic Gospels (Mt, Mk, Lk), but in Luke, it is presented in a different context which highlights our theme. The details of the parable are essentially the same in all three Gospels, and in each instance, it is followed by an interpretation of the parable for Jesus's disciples. The parable is about hearing the Word of God. Jesus explains to his disciples that the seed is the Word. The assumed farmer is Jesus himself, in this case, but will certainly apply to his disciples in the future. Jesus is delivering the Word of God generously to the people that follow him.

Unlike some cultic group or secret society, Jesus is not espousing hidden knowledge only for a select few. Luke has already told his readers in 8.1, "Jesus traveled about from one town and village to another, proclaiming the good news of the kingdom of God." This is time for proclamation, not hidden secrets. God is a God who operates in the light and expects his followers to do likewise, as he tells them in the verses immediately following his interpretation of the parable. "No one lights a lamp and hides it in a clay jar or puts it under a bed. Instead, they put it on a stand, so that those who come in can see the light. For there is nothing hidden that will not be disclosed, and nothing concealed that will not be known or brought out into the open." Then he says to them, "Therefore, consider carefully how you listen."

This latter statement is the second time in this chapter that Jesus cautions his followers about hearing what he has to say. Following the Parable of the Sower, Jesus calls out to the crowd, "Whoever has ears to hear, let them hear" (8.8), because the Parable of the Sower is about authentic hearing. In his explanation to his disciples following the telling of the parable, Jesus says that the various soils represent various people who are *hearing* the Word of God. The ground that hasn't been prepared or cultivated won't produce a crop. It must be ready to receive the seed.

While the message is spoken to everyone, not everyone will persevere in the Word long enough to produce fruit. Some, perhaps like the Pharisees and the Scribes, have hardened hearts that refuse to allow the Word to take root. Others receive the Word but lack sincerity, fall away, or perhaps allow the "worries, riches, and pleasures" of this life to rob them of spiritual fruit. No doubt, this is the reason he so stringently urges his disciples not to worry about life's needs or to accumulate riches, as these things so easily deter spiritual maturity. Remember, it is hard for a rich person to enter the kingdom of God (18.24).

Earlier I mentioned that this past summer I decided to plant a vegetable garden. The location I chose was a small plot of ground next to my house that had been part of the original landscaping. When the house was built, the landscaper had planted Yew bushes in this area and had spread landscaping rocks all around to keep weeds down and to permit drainage. In the forty years since the house was built, the Yew bushes had died and the rocks were no longer keeping the weeds at bay.

I hired a man to remove the bushes and their roots, but I was still left with a plot of ground full of rocks. Anyone who has tried to remove landscaping rocks from a garden knows that it is a nearly impossible task! I raked, shoveled, sifted, and picked by hand for a long time before I could get the ground usable for planting. Even after all of this, I am still finding rocks. However, I removed enough rocks that I could get plants to grow and actually had a very productive garden. Of course, removing the rocks was not the only thing I had to do to prepare the soil. I also added compost and fertilizer and I tilled it before it was ready to plant.

Jesus is telling the crowd and his disciples that this is the same kind of work that goes into having a heart that produces fruit when the Word is planted. It must be prepared and the soil cultivated before it can produce a crop one hundred fold. This is what it means "to have ears to hear." One's heart must be open and ready to receive but, then, also ready to act. Openness of heart is what determines if we have "ears to hear."

A disciple hears through the ears of humility to receive what direction or correction the master offers. As has already been noted, much of Jesus's kingdom teaching is counter-cultural but is also counterintuitive; in other words, it doesn't come natural to us. An obedient heart is open to the truth that choosing God's way is better than choosing our own way. As Jesus says about the ground that does produce fruit, we have to "hear the word, retain it, and by persevering produce a crop" (8.15).

This section of Luke Chapter Eight wraps up with an incident in which Jesus's mother and brothers have come to see him (8.19–21). This is a brief passage of only three verses and is an incident in the life of Jesus placed in a very different context in the other Synoptics. Luke has chosen this location, no doubt, because it brings home his motif of authentic hearing that is pervasive in this section of the Gospel.

The passage is devoid of a lot of context and seems unrelated to the preceding sections except that it carries the same theme. Jesus's mother and brothers have come to see him, but they are unable to get near him because of the crowd. Unlike in Mark, where Jesus is in a house, Luke does not tell us where Jesus is. It seems likely that Jesus's family has gotten a message to him that they would like to see him, and the implication is that he should drop everything to make them a priority.

Their request is not unreasonable, as we would not begrudge a famous public figure who gives preferential treatment to family members over the mass of fans. Jesus, however, has a very different response. He states, "My mother and brothers are those who *hear* God's word and put it into practice" (8.21 italics mine). It isn't Jesus's intention to be disrespectful to his family, but he takes this moment to define parameters around which his community, his new family, is constructed.

We have noted before that when Jesus tells his disciples to be generous to the poor, and tells the rich to invite to their table those who can't repay them, he is essentially telling them to treat everyone like family. Table fellowship and the sharing of goods are what we do with people who belong to our family. As he told his disciples in the SOP, when we are merciful and benevolent to one another, then we are indeed "children of the Most High" (6.35), and one characteristic that binds this family together is authentic hearing—"hear the Word, retain it, and by persevering produce a crop."

"This Is My Son, Listen to Him"

The authentic hearing motif climaxes in Chapter Nine with the scene of the transfiguration. While this is a climactic moment, it is not the end of the motif in the Gospel, as Luke will continue it into Chapter Ten of the travel narrative. At the beginning of Chapter Nine, Jesus sends the Twelve out on mission. The Twelve were designated apostles by Jesus in Chapter Six, and now, after some time of walking with him, listening to him, and observing his ministry, he empowers them to extend his message and ministry beyond his person. He is in effect sending them on a sort of internship but also moving toward his ultimate goal of duplicating himself in them. Acts will demonstrate that this goal is achieved as the Twelve spearhead the church's ministry and in turn multiply themselves. The disciples return after a successful ministry tour, and Jesus tries to take them aside for a respite, but the crowd learns of their whereabouts and seeks Jesus out. The result is the great story of the feeding of the 5000, which is recorded in all four Gospels.

As has already been mentioned, woven among these early episodes of Chapter Nine are questions about Jesus's identity, first from Herod and then from Jesus to his disciples. We as readers of Luke know who Jesus is, but the crowds that follow Jesus are still trying to figure him out. This tension in the narrative creates a certain heightened sense of drama that pulls us along as readers to draw the correct conclusion about who Jesus is, in case we may have our doubts or have missed the not-so-subtle hints.

Following the feeding of the 5000, Jesus takes the inner circle of his disciples, Peter, James, and John, up on the Mount of Transfiguration with him and is transformed into his glory while speaking with Moses and Elijah. A cloud engulfs the three disciples as they observe this scene and a voice announces, "This is my Son, whom I have chosen; listen to him" (9.35). This scene and the pronouncement from heaven serve as the second of two literary bookends, the first of which can be found at Jesus's baptism—"You are my Son, whom I love; with you I am well pleased" (Lk 3.22).

The pronouncement of Chapter Nine accomplishes a twofold purpose. For the reader, it releases the tension and ends the drama concerning Jesus's identity. While this is a private moment shared only with three of Jesus's disciples, this scene allows the questions about Jesus's identity finally to be put to rest. In addition, with this scene occurring in the midst of the Gospel section developing the authentic hearing motif, this message from heaven reinforces the command for Jesus's disciples to "listen to him." Jesus's teaching on discipleship is about to intensify in the travel narrative beginning in 9.51, so the need to hear and to respond to his word becomes paramount.

5

At the Master's Feet

A final scene that drives this hearing motif home is found within the travel narrative itself in the story of Mary and Martha (10.38–42). This story is unique to the Gospel of Luke as is the parable of the Good Samaritan, which precedes it. In 10.38, we are told that "as Jesus and his disciples were on their way," they come to the home of Mary and Martha. These two women are sisters, but beyond that we are not given anymore information about them. Of course, the Gospel of John reveals quite a bit more about these two devoted disciples of Jesus, and their brother Lazarus, and Jesus's close friendship with them.[6] Luke's lack of detail is likely because of his greater interest in the moral of this story over its biographical content. It's a story that lacks any real connection with its narrative surroundings, save that we are told through the introductory comment that it is part of the travel narrative.

Martha and Mary have invited Jesus and his disciples for a meal in their home. Martha is quite occupied with meal preparation, while Mary, her sister, sits at Jesus's feet to hear his teaching. We don't know if it is just the Twelve with Jesus or also the larger group of disciples, whom we were told earlier is traveling to Jerusalem with Jesus. Either way, the number of dinner guests is probably sizeable. Since first-century Palestinian women were expected to handle the domestic responsibilities, Mary and Martha had a large task before them, but one they were no doubt happy to undertake.

Hospitality in Middle Eastern culture of that day, as it is still today, is a sacred obligation. My first encounter with this kind of hospitality occurred on a trip I took to Turkey some years ago. I was sent to Turkey by the university where I was teaching to teach in a semester abroad program for our students. I was traveling with my wife, one other professor, and ten of our students. We had traveled to Antakya, Turkey, which is located near the site of ancient Syrian Antioch mentioned in the book of Acts. The professor I was traveling with happened to know a family there, and so he, my wife and I, and one or two of our students went one evening to visit them, before heading to dinner with the rest of our group. This family was part of a small group of Syrian Christians still left in this region of Turkey.

A few minutes into our visit, the woman of the house began to insist that we stay to eat dinner. We kindly declined and told her that we were going to meet the rest of our group back at the hotel to head to a restaurant. Nevertheless, she continued to insist that we stay and also invite the rest of the group to join us. Thinking this was too much for her, we continued to decline. It was clear from our surroundings that this Syrian-Turkish family barely had enough means to feed themselves, let alone our entire group. However, after her continued insistence, we relented and accepted her generous hospitality. Not wanting to place an undue burden on this kind family, my colleague and I agreed privately that we would give them the money we had budgeted to spend at the restaurant that evening.

By nine o'clock, this family had set up a long makeshift table in their living room, gathered chairs from all parts of the house (including outdoors), and had set before the thirteen of us a delicious meal. As we ate, the husband and wife of the home stood at the head of the table waiting to serve our every need. Their generosity and hospitality were so moving that it left a lasting impression on me. This is not the first time I would experience the generous hospitality of a Middle Eastern culture, but this experience in Turkey broadened my understanding of biblical stories like this one of Mary and Martha.

One can sympathize, then, when Martha comes to Jesus, a bit frustrated, and asks the Lord to make her sister Mary get up and help her prepare the meal. Luke tells us that Mary is sitting "at the Lord's feet *listening* to what he said" (emphasis mine). Martha, however, is described as "distracted by all the preparations that had to be made." The contrast between the two sisters comes to a head when Martha confronts Jesus about making her sister help her.

One interesting tidbit about this story that may or may not be of significance is that Jesus is called "Lord" three times in this narrative. Luke uses the name "Jesus" in the preceding story but, in this passage, refers to him as "Lord." Mary sits at the "Lord's feet," and Martha addresses him as "Lord." One is tempted to recall the Sermon on the Plain where Jesus says, "Why do you call me Lord, Lord and do not do what I say?" Here in this narrative, one sister, Martha, is doing, but her doing actually is keeping her from what is important and that is listening. On the other hand, Mary is listening instead of doing, which will result in informed doing of the Master's will.

Jesus commends Mary's choice when he says, "Martha, Martha, you are worried and upset about many things, but few things are needed—or indeed only one. Mary has chosen what is better, and it will not be taken away from her." We have observed in Chapter One that being at Jesus's feet is a place of encounter with him and, also, a place of repentance. For Mary it is a place of discipleship, where she learns obedience by listening to the Master. Mary, like the builder of the parable at the end of the Sermon on the Plain, is laying her foundation on bedrock.

The message to Jesus's followers, then, is that his new covenant community is comprised of disciples who hear his word and put it into practice. There is no room for hypocrisy or qualified obedience. Just as Jesus was heading to the cross in obedience to the Father, no less is expected of his disciples. We cannot put off obedience in favor of seemingly more expedient earthly demands. Not only does the story of Mary and Martha illustrate this truth, but so do the three would-be disciples found at the start of the travel narrative. Their response to Jesus's call was "First let me..." followed by responsibilities they felt outweighed the call. Fruit that results from obedient discipleship comes from spending time with the Master Gardener, who tills the soil of our hearts to respond to him. Otherwise, the demands of this life hinder the deep-rootedness that comes from hearing the Word and rob us of the joys of fruitful living.

1   The Sermon on the Plain, although much shorter, is the counterpart to Matthew's Sermon on the Mount found in Matthew 5–7. Although in both Gospels Jesus is on a mount, Luke writes that "[Jesus] went down with them [the Twelve] and stood on a level place" (6.17); and, thus, the name Sermon on the Plain. Scholars use these two designations to differentiate the two sermons.

2   See also Rom 15.8–12, where Paul quotes several prophetic passages of the gentile inclusion.

3   I'm indebted to Green and Carroll for stimulating some of the following thoughts on the SOP. Joel B. Green, *The Gospel of Luke*, NINTC (Grand Rapids: Eerdmans, 1997); John T. Carroll, *Luke: A Commentary*, TNTL (Louisville: Westminster John Knox, 2012).

4   See, for example, Carroll, *Luke*, 156; Green, *Gospel of Luke*, 280.

5   "Authentic hearing" is terminology used by Joel Green, *Gospel of Luke*, 321–23, and I am indebted to him for my understanding of this motif in Luke.

6   See John 11.1–12.11.

CHAPTER FIVE

"INCREASE OUR FAITH!"

As I begin this chapter, I feel a bit like the Apostle Paul to the Corinthians; I write it with some "fear and trembling and in much weakness" (1 Cor 2.3). The next two chapters on faith and prayer are the most daunting of all the chapters written up to this point, because I'm certainly no expert on either of these topics, but as a disciple myself, I am learning each day more about them. What is shared here is not exhaustive on these subjects, but to ignore them would be to ignore foundational elements in the life of a disciple. Faith and prayer are the points at which the disciple most closely connects with the Master, and faith is often expressed through prayer.

The impetus for considering these two subjects arises, in part, again from the uniqueness of Luke's Gospel. The only two requests that Jesus's disciples make of him in the Gospel of Luke pertain to these two subjects. In Luke 11.1, one of Jesus's disciples asks him, "Teach us to pray;" and in 17.5 they say to Jesus, "Increase our faith." The uniqueness of these requests begs the question as to what prompted the disciples to make them. Did they see something in the life and ministry of Jesus that challenged them to pursue more? Did they see how much time Jesus spent in prayer and such modeling prompted them to follow his lead? It has been well noted that Luke, more than any of the other Gospels, highlights the prayer life of Jesus and his teachings on prayer. The request to be taught how to pray seems a natural response, when perhaps the disciples see a correlation between the powerful ministry Jesus exercises and his devotion to prayer.

This in turn raises the matter of faith and the desire to have it increased. The disciples witnessed Jesus heal hundreds of people. While Luke only records a select few healing stories from Jesus's ministry, he makes evident, as do the other Gospels, that large crowds followed Jesus and many sought him out for healing. The correlation between Jesus's power-filled ministry and his devotion to regular prayer, I would suggest, is the reason for these two requests.

These requests are not only unique within Luke's Gospel, but they are also unique to Luke's Gospel. While both Matthew and Mark have some similar teachings on faith and prayer, neither presents these teachings in the same context as Luke or as requests initiated by the disciples. For example, Matthew, like Luke (but not Mark), records what we call the Lord's Prayer (LP),[1] but Matthew places it in the context of a number of other teachings in the Sermon on the Mount. In Luke, the LP is present in a context when Jesus himself is praying, which seems to prompt one of his own disciples to request that he teach them to pray. Jesus's response to the request is the Lord's Prayer, as well as additional teaching on prayer. The request to increase the disciples' faith and Jesus's subsequent response has modest similarities to passages found in both Matthew and Mark but overall is quite unique to Luke's Gospel.

I take time to elaborate a bit on the unique nature of Luke's presentation in order to emphasize once again the theme of discipleship found in his Gospel. Jesus is presented as a teacher preparing his students to carry on his ministry, which we see fulfilled in the second volume, Acts. Luke's emphasis on prayer is quite easy to trace through his Gospel and Acts, but the subject of faith is presented in a more subtle manner. The disciples clearly recognize the importance of both and, as I propose above, a connection between them.

The power of faith through prayer is intermingled with the indwelling power that comes from the Holy Spirit. Jesus had the Holy Spirit descend on him at his baptism that marked the powerful anointing of his ministry. He was, of course, also conceived by the Holy Spirit; but Luke lets us know, as well, that from the moment of his baptism, Jesus ministered in the power of God's Spirit. Luke writes, "Jesus, full of the Holy Spirit, left the Jordan and was led by the Spirit into the wilderness" (4.1); and he returned from the wilderness "in the power of the Spirit" (4.14), when he subsequently announced through Isaiah the prophet, "The Spirit of the Lord is on me" (4.18).

The return of the Spirit to Israel is a sign that the Messiah has arrived and the Spirit arrives with him. As John the Baptist told the crowd, "I baptize you with water. But one who is more powerful than I will come... He will baptize you with the Holy Spirit and fire" (3.16). The disciples share in this power when Jesus sends them out on mission in Chapter Nine, but the disciples don't tend to show consistent strength of faith and prayer until after their reception of the Spirit at Pentecost (Acts 2). Jesus chides them on more than one occasion for their lack of faith (8.25; 9.40–41). Even after returning from a mission for which he gave them power and authority to cast out demons and to heal the sick (9.1, 6), they lack the faith to feed 5000 with five loaves and two fish.

Please don't think that I am criticizing these disciples because in many ways I empathize with them. How many times has God given me power to overcome difficulty only for me to freeze before the next challenge? What we do see, if we peek ahead to Acts, is that the infilling of the Holy Spirit they receive at Pentecost transforms them into powerful ministers of the Word. Of course, the infilling of the Spirit is only icing on the cake, for it is the time they spent with Jesus that formed them into disciples who are like their teacher (Acts 4.13; cf. Lk 6.40). We will discuss more fully the importance of the infilling of the Spirit in Chapter Seven. For now, we will focus on Jesus's teaching on and demonstration of faith, and, in the next chapter, we will focus on prayer. Faith and prayer must both hang on the tool belt of every disciple who wishes to be effective like their Master.

My Story

Faith is a subtle topic in Luke and challenging to concretize; however, the reason I was drawn to it is twofold. First, it's a foregone conclusion that it is a necessary element in the life of any disciple. Second, and the one that clinched it for me, is that the request of the disciples to increase their faith is unique to Luke's Gospel. That for me, as stated earlier, begs the question, "Why?"

As mentioned in the "Introduction" to this book, part of the reason I am pursuing the topic of discipleship is for personal reasons, in order to understand better what it means to be Jesus's disciple. I have often thought a lot about faith and wondered how one connects with God through faith, particularly in the realm of healing and the miraculous. This curiosity has led me to look closely at the healing stories in the Gospels, especially Luke. I grew up in the church, so faith has always been part of my world. I've seen people receive prayer for divine healing and have been prayed for myself. I have experienced healing in my own life and have seen it in others. Yet, I am still learning what it means to connect with God through faith—that is, to move God to action as a result of faith.

My most recent experience with healing occurred this past year. I have nearly all of my life struggled with back problems. I know this is a common malady for many people, so I am sure many of you relate. In 1992, I was suffering severely with sciatic nerve pain down my right leg. God had just called my wife, Jolene, and me to church work in France; but I was bed-ridden with such pain that I was practically immobilized. I was unable to go to the upcoming mission training school we were scheduled to attend, so Jolene went without me. One night I awoke about 3:00 am with such agonizing pain that I cried out to the Lord in prayer. I said, "Lord, if you don't heal me, then I'm going to have to go to the emergency room." Since Jolene and I were, at the time, without medical insurance, or income for that matter, going to the emergency room was an expensive prospect! I only remember that I fell back to sleep, and when I awoke the next morning, I was nearly pain-free and recovered from that point forward.

That was not the end of my back problems, but I did receive a reprieve that lasted for more than two decades. In 2014, I began having pain once again down my right leg. I consulted an orthopedic surgeon who diagnosed me with a bulging disk. Physical therapy provided relief, but my back issues did not completely disappear. Over the next four years, I continued to nurse various back problems and prayed constantly for healing. I believed that God wanted to heal me, but I didn't know how to connect with him to see results. This is when my study of faith and healing really began.

One of the things I saw in the Scripture was that the people in the healing stories in the Gospels were desperate. They were at the place that, if they were not healed, they could not survive. For example, the woman with the issue of blood, who had suffered for twelve years, took to crawling through the crowd just to touch Jesus's garment. She did this despite being religiously unclean and risking moral and social judgment. She got her healing (Lk 8.43–48). Blind Bartimaeus sitting at the gate of Jericho, despite the crowd's opposition, cried out, "Jesus, Son of David, have mercy on me!" "What do you want me to do for you?", Jesus replied. He got his healing (Mk 10.46–52; cf. Lk 18.35–43).

It seems in our Western Enlightenment culture we have often discounted the power of God in favor of medicine. I'm obviously not opposed to medical care, because I believe God does use it to heal; however, sometimes it becomes a crutch for us and our hope rather than God. Prayers to God are sometimes just a layer of veneer we add to our pursuit of healing as we rely more heavily on our technological advancements.

A former student of mine and good friend, who is from Liberia in West Africa, told me once that the people there have little medical care or can't afford what there is; so the sick often come to the church for healing. Since his mother is pastor of a large charismatic church in Liberia, he has seen many miracles including the blind receiving their sight, the disabled walking, and the deaf hearing again.

Sometimes I wonder if God is waiting for us to crawl through the crowd like the bleeding woman or to cry out in desperation like

Bartimaeus. God is there and ready to give us what we seek. It never occurred to me until recently that the 3:00 am prayer in 1992 was just that—a cry of desperation. God heard and he answered. It wasn't a heroic act of faith on my part but desperation and God answered. It was not a complete healing at the time but it was a reprieve. God had better plans for me that I didn't know, at the time, but would come to understand.

My back pain returned in a major way just before Labor Day weekend in September 2018. The pain eventually became so severe that I had to return to the orthopedic surgeon's office, and an MRI was ordered which revealed a herniated disk. This was not my only problem, however, as I had also been diagnosed with two other chronic lower back issues. I spent ten days sleeping in my favorite recliner, as it was the only place I could find a relatively pain-free position. Over-the-counter pain meds along with prescription pain killers barely phased the pain. I couldn't stand or walk for more than a couple of minutes at the time. Lying flat was impossible.

The decision was made to give me an epidural injection in an attempt to relieve the pain. The injection takes about seven to ten days to work, and the medicine stays in one's system for about two weeks. Two weeks after the shot, I went back to the doctor but was still in quite a bit of pain. The shot hadn't done what it was supposed to do. It was a Friday in October when I returned to the doctor, and the next day, Saturday, I was on the phone with my brother-in-law and my two sisters. My wife and I had agreed to a scheduled conference call to spend some time in prayer with them concerning a ministry that they were about to undertake in Europe. The younger of my two sisters was already in Europe, and my older sister and her husband were in Florida preparing to join her.

My brother-in-law brought to our prayer time a Scripture reading that had impressed him. It is found in 1 Chronicles 16 where David appoints some of the Levites to worship and sing before the Lord in the tabernacle. Recorded in this chapter is a sample song of praise that they sang when ministering, which extols the Lord for who he is and his great works on behalf of Israel. Curiously, near the end of this twenty-nine-verse psalm is just one prayer request in 16.35, followed by a closing thanksgiving.

We decided to practice this pattern in our prayer time, and so we began to worship the Lord and extol what he had done in our lives. Being aware of the trial I was experiencing with my back, at one point in the prayer time. my brother-in-law began to pray for the healing of my back and was immediately joined by the rest of the group. I was still in quite a bit of pain at the time and appreciated the prayer.

After that Saturday, on the following Monday, I was spending some quiet time with the Lord, as I do most mornings. I decided that I would do what we had done on Saturday and spend some time in worship. As I did, I began to sense in my own spirit that God was speaking to me. It was not an audible voice, but an internal voice I have often heard at key moments in my life. Accompanying the voice was a strong sense that I had received my healing! I can't explain it; maybe it was a gift of faith, but I just knew I had been healed. The odd thing was that I was still in pain; but I heard that unmistakable voice inside say to me, "I have heard your petition and have granted your request."

That Monday was one of the most physically painful up to that point. Talk about a test of faith! However, I clung to what I had heard. Tuesday morning I awoke with about 85% of my pain gone! It was a major turn-around and the best I had felt since September. As the weeks passed, I continued to cling to that word from the Lord even though at times its fulfillment seemed protracted. My healing was not an instantaneous one but a gradual one that seemed accelerated over the timetable the doctors had given me. The doctors told me six to nine months, but I was seeing healing in six to nine weeks!

After the healing began, I went from trying to control my pain with prescription drugs to taking a couple of over-the-counter pain relievers per day. Within about two weeks of doing that, I started not needing pain relievers at all and returned to exercising in the gym, something that was previously impossible. As the New Year dawned in 2019, I haven't needed pain relievers, except on occasion, as I return to a normal lifestyle.

My own experience with healing has bolstered my faith and has encouraged me to believe for others. I'm still a novice at understanding how to connect with God in faith, but I am learning. I think part of the disciple's journey is to grow in faith, and the desire to grow might partly explain the disciples' request to increase their faith. It's interesting that Jesus's response to their request is not to wave his hand and somehow turn up the rheostat of their faith, so that it burns more brightly; he simply told them the power of what just a little faith could do. "If you have faith as small as a mustard seed, you can say to this mulberry tree, 'Be uprooted and planted in the sea,' and it will obey you" (Lk 17.6). Jesus's response is that faith is not about quantity but quality. All we need is a little genuine faith to move mountains or uproot a mulberry tree, but why does it seem so difficult to have even that? I believe that the key to having this kind of faith is developing greater intimacy with God. This is where prayer and faith intersect.

Faith Is Recognizing Jesus

The first way that we connect with God in faith is through salvation. That is the encounter I speak of in Chapter One. Most believers take it for granted that God will answer the sincere prayer of a repentant sinner. Jesus illustrates this truth in the parable of the Pharisee and the Tax Collector in Luke 18.9–14 and states in Luke 5.32 that "I have not come to call the righteous but sinners to repentance." Why is our faith so strong for this answer to prayer? Because we believe it to be God's greatest desire to save the sinner, and there are so many promises in the Scripture to support such a notion. After all, isn't that what the cross is all about?

It seems that there are three principles at work here. First, we believe without a doubt that it is God's will to save sinners. Second, we believe, because we know that God has promised it through his Word. Third, we believe because we have experienced such a salvation act ourselves and we have also witnessed it in others. We have seen the change that comes through a sincere encounter with God.

Then, why do we struggle so often to believe God for other things in our lives that we ask for in prayer? The number one reason is that we are not certain that what we are asking for is God's desire for us, and even if we do believe that God has promised it to us, we struggle to believe without a doubt that he will keep his Word. James writes, "But when you ask, you must believe and not doubt, because the one who doubts is like a wave of the sea, blown and tossed by the wind" (1.6).

There are numerous promises that God will respond to our prayers. The Gospel and First Epistle of John are full of them, and we can find them in Luke as well. For example, John writes, "Dear friends, if our hearts do not condemn us, we have confidence before God and receive from him anything we ask, because we keep his commands and do what pleases him" (1 John 3.21–22). We will explore the passages in Luke in the next chapter, but suffice it to say that Jesus teaches his disciples that their Heavenly Father is more than ready and willing to respond to their requests (Lk 11.5–13; 18.1–8).

Jesus doesn't actually separate saving faith from any other kinds of faith. The salvation of one's soul and the healing of the body are one in the same thing. The story of the healing of the paralytic best illustrates this concept (Lk 5.17–26). When the four friends of the paralyzed man pull back the roof tiles and let him down in front of Jesus, Luke writes that Jesus seeing their faith tells the paralytic, "Friend, your sins are forgiven." This statement elicited murmuring from the religious leaders, as they questioned Jesus's right and ability to forgive sins, since that is the prerogative of God. Jesus asks them, "Which is easier: to say, 'Your sins are forgiven,' or to say, 'Get up and walk'? But I want you to know that the Son of Man has authority on earth to forgive sins." He then turns to the paralytic and tells him to get up, take up his mat, and go home, which he subsequently does.

This story of the paralytic is the first in a series of what are often called conflict stories in Luke. In each story, beginning with the paralytic, Jesus's authority or way of conducting his ministry is challenged repeatedly by the religious leaders. In the next story, he is questioned as to why he eats with "tax collectors and sinners" (5.30); and after that, he is challenged as to why he doesn't fast and pray regularly like the disciples of John the

Baptist do and those of the Pharisees (5.33). Finally, his interpretation of Sabbath observance is challenged, when the Pharisees spot his disciples picking grain on the Sabbath to assuage their hunger. After letting them know that God's commands are to be a benefit to his children rather than a burden, Jesus tells them, "The Son of Man is Lord of the Sabbath" (6.5).

Luke doesn't leave us at this point but completes this series of conflict stories with a second miracle. This time, the healing takes place on the Sabbath in the synagogue right in front of the religious leaders. We are already aware from the previous encounter of their displeasure over Jesus's version of Sabbath keeping, and now Jesus challenges them once again when he heals a man with a shriveled hand. Jesus says to the Pharisees and the teachers of the law, "I ask you, which is lawful on the Sabbath: to do good or to do evil, to save life or to destroy it" (6.9)? Jesus answers his own question by healing the man. "The Pharisees and the teachers of the law were furious and began to discuss with one another what they might do to Jesus" (6.11).

What these stories illustrate, particularly because of Luke's grouping of them, is that Jesus is a person of authority; in fact, he carries God's authority. This is why the people in Capernaum marveled, because Jesus spoke as one with authority (Lk 4.32, 36). Luke doesn't record another healing story until the beginning of Chapter Seven, at which time Jesus heals the servant of a Roman centurion (7.1–10). This story provides a finishing touch to the questioning of Jesus's authority begun in Chapter Five.

In this story, the centurion has heard about Jesus and sends some of the Jewish leaders to ask Jesus to come and heal his servant. Jesus agrees and when he is not far from the centurion's house, the centurion sends some of his own servants to say, "Lord, don't trouble yourself, for I do not deserve to have you come under my roof... but say the word, and my servant will be healed" (7.6–7). Jesus is amazed at this Gentile's faith and tells the crowd that he hasn't seen this kind of faith not even in Israel (7.9). The contrast is clear that Jesus's own people, the people of God, have not so clearly recognized his authority, like this gentile soldier has. It is the recognition of Jesus's authority that gets the healing the centurion seeks.

This story is key in understanding the role of faith in the disciple's life. Faith is recognizing who Jesus is. This series of healing stories started out with Jesus's authority to forgive sins questioned but affirmed by an astounding miracle. A paralyzed man got off of his bed and walked away. It ended with a Gentile who only had heard about Jesus yet recognized that he is a man with authority. What he commands will be done. This brings us full circle to our earlier discussion of saving faith.

For Jesus, healing a person and forgiving their sins are one in the same act. He has the authority to do both, and one is no different from the other. It isn't surprising then that one of the Greek words used for healing is also the same word used for Your faith has saved/healed (sōzō, σῴζω). Four times in Luke, Jesus says to individuals, three for healing and one for forgiveness of sins, "Your faith has saved/healed (sōzō, σῴζω) you" (7.50; 8.48; 17.19; 18.42). Jesus came to set the captive free, to give sight to the blind, and to announce the time of God's favor (Lk 4.18, 19). We live in that time. Our Enlightenment mind-set tends to divide matters of the body, mind, and spirit, but Jesus does not. He heals the whole person. He is as quick to forgive sins as he is to heal sickness in a person. In fact, he wants to do both because that is the nature of the kingdom. The kingdom of God is about invading the strong man's house and taking away his goods (Lk 11.21–22). We are the "goods" that God seeks to rescue. Darkness has brought sin and sickness onto the world and Jesus brings light and life.

Faith as a Journey

Faith for the disciples was an up-and-down journey. The key word here is journey. As they walked with Jesus, they observed, experienced, and eventually learned what it looked like to have faith that would in the end uproot a mulberry tree (17.6). Even they, at times, failed to recognize who was in their presence. The story of the calming of the storm is illustrative of this failure.

In a brief account found in 8.22–25, Jesus gets into a boat on the lake of Galilee and says to his disciples, "Let's go over to the other side of the lake." Since several of them were experienced fisherman and had lived on the lake all of their lives, traveling across the lake was a normal occurrence. While navigating across the lake, however, a fierce storm arises that seemed to threaten their very lives. Jesus is in the stern of the boat asleep and oblivious to the present danger. The disciples awake Jesus and announce, no doubt in panic and with some amazement at his soundness of sleep, "Master, Master, we're going to die!" (translation mine). Jesus got up and calmed the wind and the waves and then asked them one simple question, "Where is your faith?"

While this story may seem like a failure for the disciples, it gives me hope. It lets me know that my occasional lack of faith is *ok* but also that learning to have faith is a journey. In that moment of panic, the disciples forgot who was on the journey with them. Faith is recognizing who Jesus is, like the Centurion, but sometimes we forget. Panic can have that effect.

Luke writes in the next verse, "In fear and amazement they asked one another, 'Who is this? He commands even the winds and the water, and they obey him.'" This story is, of course, part of the section of the Gospel we spoke about previously in which Jesus's identity is in question; however, this verse also speaks to the journey of faith. Faith is recognizing who Jesus is, and in order to do that, we must come to know him. We must spend time with him.

The disciples' up-and-down journey continues in Luke Chapter Nine. At the beginning of the chapter, Jesus gives them "power and authority to drive out all demons and to cure diseases" (9.1); and they went out "proclaiming the good news and healing people everywhere" (9.6). This was the disciples' internship as they went out to practice what they had seen their Master do. Although Luke doesn't elaborate, it appears that the disciples had a successful mission; and Jesus drew them aside, likely for some rest and further instruction. There are two other episodes that follow in this chapter that reveal that the disciples, despite their successful mission, are still struggling in their faith.

Following the disciples' return, the people in the region learned where Jesus had gone and followed him into the wilderness where he had retreated with the disciples. Jesus welcomed them, healed their sickness, and taught them about the kingdom. At the end of the day, the disciples wanted him to send the people away, so that they could go to the surrounding towns and find food. Instead, Jesus presents them with a faith challenge (or opportunity) and tells them to provide the crowd with food.

One would think that after receiving authority to drive out demons and to heal the sick, the disciples would have this faith thing all figured out; however, their response is to see the impossibility rather than the possibility of the situation. "We have only five loaves of bread and two fish—unless we go and buy food for all this crowd" (9.13). Their eyes are on their limitations and not on recognizing who is in their presence.

I have to say, again, please don't think that I am criticizing the disciples; but I am learning from them and empathizing with them! We are encouraged and blessed to know what the end of this journey looks like for them—they become unstoppable people of faith! This should be an inspiration to all of us in our journey.

The second episode in Chapter Nine follows the transfiguration. When Jesus and the three disciples, Peter, James, and John, come down from the mount, Jesus encounters a father who pleads with him to deliver his son from demonic oppression that is causing him to convulse and foam at the mouth. The father tells Jesus, "I begged your disciples to drive it out, but they could not" (9.40). "You unbelieving and perverse generation," Jesus replied, "how long shall I stay with you and put up with you? Bring your son here" (9.41). Again, this moment in the text is following a time when the disciples have experienced enough faith to cast out demons and to heal the sick. While it isn't possible to affirm that this incident occurred after the disciples had returned from mission, Luke presents it that way in the chronology of the story.

Jesus mildly rebukes his disciples one other time, later in the Gospel, when he is teaching them about concern over daily necessities like food and clothing. He says to them, "If that is how God clothes the grass of the field, which is here today, and tomorrow is thrown into the fire, how much more will he clothe you—you of little faith!" (12.28). Jesus isn't disappointed in the disciples, but wants them to recognize to whom they belong. God is both their Heavenly Father and creator who cares for their needs. So, he tells them not to be like everyone else who spends their waking hours worrying about and toiling for such needs, but focus instead on the kingdom and "these things will be given to you as well" (12.31).

Where Do We Go from Here?

While the disciples' faith journey, much like ours, is an up-and-down one, they do seem to have found an eventual consistency that launched them into a powerful ministry. There are two key elements to this transformation that we will explore in the remainder of this book. The first key element is the reception of the promised Holy Spirit, which was not only transformational but also empowering. Like their "internship mission," the disciples receive Jesus's authority to cast out demons and to heal the sick. The difference is that this power now resides with them permanently, as the Spirit of Jesus (Acts 16.7) takes up residence in them. As John the Baptist had prophesied that Jesus would "baptize you with the Holy Spirit and fire" (Lk 3.16c), Jesus instructs his disciples, "I am going to send you what my Father has promised; but stay in the city until you have been clothed with power from on high" (Lk 24.49)—a promise he reiterates in Acts 1.4–5. We will explore this empowerment in more detail in Chapter Seven.

The second key element to the disciples' transformation on display in Acts can be found in Acts 4.13. Luke records the following reflections concerning the Jewish ruling council in Jerusalem, "When they saw the courage of Peter and John and realized that they were unschooled, ordinary men, they were astonished and they took note that these men had been with Jesus." Since faith is recognizing who Jesus is, it comes from spending time with him just as he did with the Father. Spending time with Jesus is the answer to the request, "Increase our faith" (Lk 17.5). The way we do that is through prayer; and this is where prayer and faith intersect, and it is at this point we will turn to explore the subject of prayer as presented in the Gospel of Luke.

[1]   Also referred to as *Pater Noster* from the Latin, "Our Father."

CHAPTER SIX

"Lord, Teach Us to Pray"

"At 15, it felt as if my life were over. My dreams were just a joke. I sank deeper into despair," writes Lauren Daigle, a popular Christian crossover artist, who wrote the cover story in *Guideposts* magazine recounting her own struggle with a debilitating illness and how prayer brought her through.[1] Lauren contracted what everyone thought was mononucleosis; however, her symptoms seemed to get much worse, and eventually she found herself completely lacking energy and nearly unable to function on a daily basis. She writes, "I was so exhausted that I couldn't even lift the remote to change the channel." After a long and arduous process of tests and doctors' appointments, she was diagnosed with cytomegalovirus, a more debilitating form of mono.

Lauren shares how day-to-day life became an impossible chore, during which time she was completely dependent on her family for daily necessities. She speaks of the utter despair that swept over her, "Why was this happening? Would I be like this for the rest of my life? What kind of life would that be? No life at all." In her desperate attempt to find solace and answers to her questions, she recounts how, after everyone in the house left for their daily activities, she would literally crawl up to a loft in their house, where she would spend quiet time with God in prayer.

She said, "It was my secret place, my prayer closet." Prayer was the key to overcoming her hopelessness and regaining her life; this quiet place became a place of refuge for her where she met with God. It wasn't about the amount of time she spent, at one point she writes, "Mom had bought a devotional on sale someplace: *One Minute of Praise*, the book was called. That is about all I was good for. One minute." It was about her consistency, "I read that five-dollar devotional and listened for God's voice. Day after day, I kept going back to the loft, struggling up the stairs, pausing on each step to catch my breath. I'd always had a strong faith. Or thought I did. Now it was being tested beyond endurance."

During these two years of suffering, she asked God what he wanted to do with her life. He began to reveal his plan to her through an unusual vision of herself singing to thousands, traveling on a tour bus, and writing and producing her own music. These were all things she had never yet done, but are all things she is doing today. She laid the foundation for this life of music ministry during those private prayer times with God.

Jesus's Prayer Life

As Lauren demonstrates, consistent prayer and communion with God is a key part of a disciple's life. Jesus modeled this kind of prayer life for his disciples. Luke seems to have noticed this as well, since he highlights more than any other Gospel, Jesus's practice of and teachings on prayer. Luke's presentation of Jesus's consistent commitment to personal prayer is subtle yet discernable in the Gospel. For example, Jesus is often said to be praying at key moments in his life such as at his baptism (3.21), before choosing the twelve disciples (6.12), and on the mount, before he is transfigured (9.29). When Jesus teaches the disciples the Lord's Prayer, it is itself found in the context of a prayer moment in Jesus's life (11.1). This consistent portrayal of Jesus at prayer merely affirms what Luke tells his readers early in his presentation of Jesus's ministry that "Jesus often withdrew to lonely places and prayed" (5.16).

While Matthew and Mark record these events in Jesus's life, neither of them makes a point to say that Jesus is praying before or during these moments. The fact that Matthew and Mark lack these references does not discredit them in any way. It is a matter of emphasis and a choice made by Luke to highlight an area of Jesus's life that he evidently finds important. He demonstrates this commitment to prayer was passed on to the disciples, who are also found praying at key moments in their lives, for example, following the first persecution (Acts 4.24–31) or when designating the first missionaries (Acts 13.2–3). Like Jesus, the early believers also "devoted themselves... to prayer" (Acts 2.42).

In addition to demonstrating that it was Jesus's habit to pray, Luke also emphasizes Jesus's teaching on prayer. There are two Lukan passages of particular importance for our topic, both because of the teaching they contain and because they are unique to Luke. They are Luke 11.1–13 and 18.1–8. We will tackle Luke 11.1–13 first, in an attempt to understand what Jesus wants his disciples to know about the power of prayer.

In Luke 11.1–13, Jesus is praying when one of his disciples requests, "Lord, teach us to pray, just as John taught his disciples" (11.1). The "John" referred to here is, of course, John the Baptist, who also had followers. In fact, when the Pharisees criticize Jesus and his disciples for not fasting regularly, their examples for good behavior are their own disciples and those of John the Baptist (Lk 5.33). Fasting and praying were part of the regular regimen for devout Jews, so teaching one's disciples to pray was fundamental.

What is curious here is that the request is initiated by a disciple. One would expect that Jesus would have included prayer instruction as part of his ongoing training, and therefore such a request would be unnecessary. No doubt Jesus did include prayer as part of his training or Luke would not have given it such emphasis; however, having the request on the lips of a disciple helps remind us that what is about to be taught is important to discipleship.

There are two parts to the prayer teaching in Luke 11.1–13. They are the model prayer, usually called the Lord's Prayer (LP), or what some have called, perhaps more accurately, the Disciple's Prayer and the subsequent teaching on a disciple's attitude in prayer. It isn't my intention to analyze in detail the LP here, but to simply highlight what Jesus's overall message is to his disciples about prayer. The LP, as it is recorded in Luke, is a shorter version than the one found in Matthew and, as has been noted previously, is in a different context from Matthew. There are, however, key elements present in the prayer that are consistent with Jesus's teaching as portrayed in Luke.[2]

The Lord's Prayer

The LP begins with the address, "Our Father," which features, from the start, the role prayer plays in the ongoing development of the disciple's intimate relationship with God. Jesus's own relationship to God has been portrayed consistently throughout the Gospel of Luke as Son to Father (e.g., 1.32; 2.49; 3.22). Jesus's intimate relationship with God as Father is expressed in his own prayers (10.21 (2x); 23.34, 46) and would have certainly been noticed by his disciples. Twice when Jesus was praying, the Father speaks of him as "my Son, whom I love; with [whom] I am well pleased" (3.22) and "my Son, whom I have chosen" (9.35). In addition, Jesus speaks regularly of God as their Father in his teachings to his disciples (6.36; 9.26; 10.22; 12.32; 11.13; 12.32).

The portrayal of God as "Father" emphasizes his merciful and loving care for the disciples and affirms the familial nature of the community that Jesus is forming (8.21). Although addressing God as Father in Jewish prayer[3] is not unprecedented, a number of scholars agree that behind the Greek term for "father," here, lies the more intimate Aramaic title for father, *Abba*. *Abba* is found elsewhere in the New Testament[4] and expresses an intimacy with God that is less common in first-century Jewish religious circles.

"Your kingdom come" is the first request of the Father and is a prayer for the establishment of justice in the world. Justice and righteousness are fairly interchangeable terms in the Bible as both are often translated from the same Hebrew and Greek words. For God, righteousness is not a philosophical or theological concept, but it implies walking according to his commands, which includes caring for the vulnerable and marginalized of society—the poor, the orphans, and the widows (Ex 22.22). Among the many indictments against Israel in the Old Testament was that they "[grind] the faces of the poor" (Isa 3.15) and take advantage of the powerless.

Jesus's announcement of the arrival of the kingdom and the Year of Jubilee is tantamount to proclaiming a new exodus (Lk 9.31) for the oppressed. This is good news for the poor, the captive, and the oppressed for, like enslaved Israel in Egypt, God has heard their cry and remembered his covenant with Abraham, Isaac, and Jacob (Ex 2.24; Lk 1.54–55, 72). The arrival of the kingdom, however, is still in an "already and not yet"[5] phase of its presence, as oppression and injustice continue in the world. The kingdom was present in Jesus's ministry and is present in the community of his Spirit which he left behind. The responsibility of this community of disciples is to spread the good news of the kingdom on earth, to fight injustice, and to pray for the coming of the kingdom, both now and in fullness when Jesus returns.

When Jesus sent out the twelve (9.1–6) and the seventy-two on mission (10.1–7), he told them not to take anything for their journey, but their reliance was to be on the provision of their Father. In Luke 12.22–34, Jesus tells his disciples that their daily needs for food and clothing are known to their Father and that they are not to worry or pursue these things. They are to pursue, instead, the kingdom of God, "and these things will be given to you as well." The second request in the LP, then, is for our daily needs, "give us each day our daily bread." Provision is part of what a disciple can expect from God, which is, perhaps, reminiscent of the Israelites' dependence on God for their daily bread (manna) in the wilderness.

The Lord's Prayer rounds out with a request for forgiveness of our own sins, as we continue to forgive others. Jesus has already taught his disciples that the nature of his community is to be one characterized by forgiveness of each other (6.37), which is simply living out the nature of the Father himself, "because he is kind to the ungrateful and wicked" (6.35). Jesus, as always, leads by example, for his final prayer in Luke is for his executioners, "Father, forgive them for they do not know what they are doing" (23.34). The LP ends with the request, "lead us not into temptation"[6] (11.4), which likely expresses the desire that the Father protect his children from anything that would cause them to stray from the righteous path.

The Parable of the Inopportune Friend

The parable and teaching that follow the model prayer reinforce the notion that God the Father desires his children to pray, and that their expectation should be that he is ready and willing to fulfill every request. Jesus tells a parable about two neighbors in a village, who are also close friends, one of whom has an unexpected traveler arriving at his home late one evening. (We discussed in a previous chapter the importance of hospitality in the Middle East, which means the host is under obligation to provide food and shelter for his traveling friend.) Not having anything to set before the traveler, the host runs next door and knocks on his neighbor's door to see if he can borrow some food.

We must remember that this is not a neighborhood situation best known to us, and running down the street to the 24-hour convenience store is not an option. This is a first-century Palestinian village where everyone knows everyone and the obligations of hospitality are always fulfilled. As noted before, this is a shame and honor culture in which it is important to fulfill one's obligation to one's family or community. In addition, living in the house where the host goes to borrow food is not just a casual neighbor but a community friend.[7] Jesus, of course as is his custom, provides details in the story that are either outlandish or are on the edge of propriety, in order to make his point as powerful as possible.

He describes the host going to his friend's house at midnight and knocking on the door to ask for food. Friend or not, shame and honor notwithstanding, this so-called friend is asking a lot of his neighbor to get up in the middle of the night to loan him food. Even in our culture, we wouldn't imagine disturbing our neighbor in the middle of the night for any reason except a dire emergency, much less to borrow some bread. This, however, is exactly Jesus's point. Nobody would welcome this scenario, and everyone understands the neighbor's unwillingness to get up and give his friend what he wants.

Like the householder in the story, we would all want to tell him to go away and for good reason. Jesus, however, knows the culture of the disciples he addresses. He assures them that this inconvenienced friend and neighbor will get up and give his friend whatever he asks for, because cultural obligations demand it. He knows to turn his friend away would bring shame, not only on himself, but also on his friend, who is in turn under obligation to the hungry traveler back home.[8]

The point of the parable is to demonstrate that if we as humans will grant requests, not so much out of good will, but simply out of obligation, then how much more a loving God will grant our prayerful petitions. So, Jesus urges his disciples to "ask… seek… knock… and it will be given to you for… everyone who asks receives." Jesus pushes forward his point further by comparing God to earthly fathers. He concludes by saying, "If you then, though you are evil, know how to give good gifts to your children, how much more will your Father in heaven give the Holy Spirit to those who ask him!" (11.13).[9] Jesus is teaching his disciples about God's willingness to respond to prayer. In the next passage we will consider, known as the Parable of the Unjust Judge and the Widow (Lk 18.1–8), Jesus teaches his disciples about not only God's willingness to respond but also the importance of persistence in prayer.

The Parable of the Unjust Judge and the Widow

The Parable of the Unjust Judge and the Widow, like the Parable of the Inopportune Friend, is unique to Luke's Gospel. This parable of a persistent widow is told by Jesus to his disciples in order to teach them that "they should always pray and not give up" (18.1). The focus of this story is a cry for justice by a widow who lives in an unspecified community. In this same community lives a judge, whom Jesus says "neither feared God nor cared what people thought." The widow continually comes to the judge with the plea, "Grant me justice against my adversary." The contrast in the story is clear and the hyperbole certain. The two characters in the story represent the extremes of the social hierarchy and pit the powerless against the powerful.

One place the hyperbole in this parable is most obvious is in the characterization of the judge. He is essentially despicable. A person who doesn't fear God or care about what people think is a person who has no moral restraint. In the religious world of first-century Judaism, to be a person that doesn't fear God is reprehensible. God's law concerns itself with two basic elements—the fear of God and love of our fellow human being. This judge is devoid of both, which makes him an unrighteous and an unjust judge.

The judge in this story represents the counterpart to and also the antithesis of God. It is through the stark contrast and absurd characterization of the judge that Jesus will make his point. Since the judge is amoral, he doesn't have to grant the widow's request, and even in an honor/shame culture where he might feel societal pressure to do so, he does not. Remember, he doesn't care what people think!

The widow represents us in the parable. By making the petitioner the powerless and most undeserving person of society (not in God's eyes of course), Jesus develops a character in the story that could represent any petitioner. Widows figure prominently in the Lukan narrative and are usually listed as part of the class of poor and vulnerable in the Old Testament. In a day when social security was nonexistent, widows were quite financially vulnerable and, in a male-dominated society, leaned heavily on the men in their lives.

The widow pleads for justice against her adversary. The Greek term translated for "adversary" in the petition is also used of Satan in 1 Peter 5.8 and, in general, means "accuser" or "enemy."[10] Although the term generally means any enemy or adversary, it shouldn't be lost on us that such a plea could mimic a prayer of God's children against their adversary, the Devil. After all, the entire parable is about being persistent in prayer, and the focus of the widow's plea is justice.

We spoke above about how justice and righteousness are often derived from the same Hebrew and Greek word. These two concepts are inescapably linked in God's kingdom. Jesus's setting free of the captives and the oppressed is about bringing justice to those bound by Satan's power. Anything unjust in this world is unrighteous in God's sight, and it is the responsibility of the community of Jesus's followers to pray for his kingdom (i.e., justice) to come.

Justice and the Coming Kingdom

Jesus is teaching his disciples that praying for the kingdom to come is to pray for the works of the Devil to be reversed and for those, who have all their lives been bound, to be set free. We all have various views of what injustice looks like, but I am painting with a broad brush here. Sickness, suffering, human trafficking, slavery, poverty, bullying, and I could go on are all injustices, and they spring from the realm of darkness. These are the things against which Jesus tells his followers to pray. The goal of these prayers is the advancement of the kingdom of God until the coming of the Son of Man.

It's important to note that this parable about persistence or, perhaps more rightly stated, perseverance in prayer falls at the end of a section about the kingdom and the coming of the Son of Man. The section begins back at Luke 17.20, where Luke states that Jesus's remarks are prompted by a question from the Pharisees about when the kingdom of God would come. The Pharisees' expectation of how the kingdom would come, and what it would look like, is quite different from what Jesus is proclaiming. They were no doubt looking for a restoration of the throne of David, the deliverance of Israel from foreign domination, and the return of the rule of God's law as they interpreted it.

Concern for the poor or marginalized was not likely utmost on their minds, and they certainly expected to be at the center of any power brokering that would be done in the new kingdom. Jesus tells them that the kingdom is not seen with the physical eye but with the eyes of the Spirit, "because the kingdom of God is in your midst" (17.21). Every day in their midst, through the power of the kingdom present in Jesus, justice is replacing injustice, and the kingdom is tangibly advancing in the lives of those whom Jesus sets free (cf. 7.20–22).

Jesus, then, turns to his disciples and tells them, "The time is coming when you will long to see one of the days of the Son of Man, but you will not see it" (17.22). Therefore, he urges them in the interim period to persevere and not to be led astray by others. He told the Pharisees that "The coming of the kingdom is not something that can be observed" (17.20), but tells his disciples that the coming of the Son of Man will be as obvious as lightning that flashes from one part of the sky to the other. Before then, however, he must suffer and they must persevere. For their faith not to go all the way to the end is like Lot's wife who looked back, while running from Sodom, and became a pillar of salt (17.32). His coming will be the visible establishment of the rule of God and will consummate what began in his ministry. His coming is the fulfillment of the "already and not yet" of the kingdom.

Jesus finishes his admonition to perseverance with the parable of the widow and the unjust judge. His instruction to the disciples is to persist in prayer to God, for the reversal of injustice in the world and for the defeat of their adversary, the Devil. Through this exaggerated tale set in this unknown community, Jesus encourages his disciples that God will indeed hear their prayer and answer it. Just like the unjust judge, who doesn't fear God or care about what people think, gives justice to this widow, "will not God bring about justice for his chosen ones?" (18.7).

Jesus tells his disciples to "listen to what the unjust judge says" (18.6). The judge in the parable grants the request of the widow, not because he is worn down by her coming, but because he is afraid that she might do something worse to him than just bug him! Many English translations fail to catch the nuance here, the hyperbole of the story, and simply translate the text by having the judge grant her request "because she keeps bothering me" (18.5).[11] However, the judge has already endured countless days of the same request. The Greek word used here, *hupōpiazō* (ὑπωπιάζω), likely means something stronger, like blackening his eye or striking him in the face.[12] This interpretation would be in line with the overall exaggerated elements in the story and also with Jesus's teaching style. How could a widow give a judge and prominent member of society a black eye?!

The absurdity of the story sets up the disciples, and us, for Jesus to drive home his point. The judge's granting the widow's request is based on nothing more than his own self-preservation. In contrast, Jesus presents the loving and generous response of the Father to his children as quick and decisive. This is the "how much more" *a fortiori* style argument we have seen before.

The tension here in this entire passage beginning in 17.20 through this parable's conclusion is the sense of delay and longing to see the coming of the Son of Man. The disciples must have the faith to believe that even though it seems like God is not hearing their prayers for justice and his coming kingdom, he does and will act swiftly to respond to them. The question that Jesus leaves with his disciples and us by extension is, "When the Son of Man comes will he find faith on the earth?" (18.8).

It's important that we understand this question in light of the context. The English translation once again fails us a bit here. In the Greek text, there is an article in front of the word "faith" and, thus, when literally translated would be "the faith." However, in English we don't tend to use articles in front of abstract nouns like faith, unless we wish to speak of a certain type of faith. We might say, for example, "the faith of a child" or "the faith of our ancestors." In this context, we would not normally say, "When the Son of Man comes will he find *the* faith on the earth?"

Greek uses articles differently from English, and it is the intention here in the Greek text to speak of a particular faith, not just any faith at all. Jesus is asking his disciples if when he (the Son of Man) returns, he will find this kind of persistent faith that calls on God for the justice of the coming kingdom. Unlike Lot's wife, will their faith go all the way to the end? And even though there seems to be no end in sight and their suffering seems to endure, will they believe that God will answer their prayers? These are the questions that linger for every contemporary disciple nearly 2000 years later.

What We Have Learned

It seems that we can draw out three principles from Luke's presentation of prayer. First, he highlights the importance of prayer in Jesus's life and ministry by noting his consistency in spending time with the Father, "Jesus often withdrew to lonely places, and prayed" (5.16). Key moments in his life are moments at which he is communing with the Father, such as at his baptism and when he chooses the Twelve. Second, Jesus's prayer life encourages his disciples to learn to pray. Jesus teaches them not only a model prayer, but to expect that God wishes to hear and grant their requests, "Ask and you shall receive." Third, even if God doesn't respond on their time schedule, he will respond with justice and quickly for those who persist in prayer, "When the Son of Man comes will he find *the* faith on the earth?"

This final question brings us back to the union of prayer and faith or faithfulness. Prayer is where the disciple finds intimacy with God and grows in the knowledge of who God is. Prayer is the tool through which faith operates, and faith is what moves the heart of God. Lauren Daigle learned this lesson over the course of two years of great suffering. Though her body was weakened, her faith was strengthened, and it was her consistency in prayer and faith expressed to God that she found the powerful music ministry she now enjoys.

I too learned the importance of consistency through a difficult trial in my own life. I shared with you at the beginning of Chapter One how I came to the Lord after the passing of my father. It was a profound experience of salvation, but what I didn't share with you was the difficulties of the year and a half that followed. It was the most challenging time of my journey with Christ. I got involved in my church youth group, and everyone saw me as a wonderful Christian; but I knew better. Keeping up the façade of being a good church-going Christian while knowing things were not right between God and me became a burden impossible for me to bear.

After I stopped trying to hide my duplicity, confessing my failings and frustrations to my mother, and more importantly to God, my life got back on track. I came to realize that there was a major element missing from my life that had robbed me of a successful journey with Christ, and that was simply spending time with God. No one had taken time to instruct me on what it meant to be a disciple, and I didn't know that I was supposed to spend time with God every day! Apparently, everyone just thought I knew everything I needed to know and was good to go. After all, I was raised in a pastor's home! Such assumptions are dangerous for any new believer. Over the years, I have found that making disciples, which is part of the Great Commission (Matt 28.19), is something that many churches don't do well.

From the point I rededicated my life to Christ, I began reading the Bible regularly and spending time in prayer. I won't say that I was terribly good at it in the beginning, but one evening the Lord spoke to me so clearly and admonished me not to forsake my time with him. From that point forward, I made sure that I read the Bible every day, and I would spend thirty minutes in prayer. I don't necessarily recommend that everyone do what I did, but I wanted to show the Lord my commitment. So, even though my mind would wander at times, and I might not know what to say, I would sit in his presence for at least thirty minutes. It wasn't easy at first, but it eventually became a habit and finally a desire.

I look forward to my time with the Lord these days. In the beginning, I had my devotions at night but found I was often too tired, or they got pushed off by other events. For years now, they have been the first thing I do to start my day, and I believe that God has honored that time with him. Jesus says in Matthew 6.6, "But when you pray, go into your room, close the door and pray to your Father, who is unseen. Then your Father, who sees what is done in secret, will reward you." So whatever you can do and whatever time you can offer God in prayer, he will reward. It is just a matter of being consistent and having faith in him that he will do what he promises. It is consistent prayer and faith in God that every disciple needs and forms the foundation for the empowered life. The empowered life is the subject of the next chapter.

1   Lauren Daigle, "Known to Me," *Guideposts* (Feb 2019), 24–28.

2   Joel Green, *The Gospel of Luke*, NINTC (Grand Rapids: Eerdmans, 1997), 440.

3   There are a number of Scriptures in the Old Testament that address the fatherhood of God (e.g., Deut 14.1; 2 Sam 7.14; Ps 2.7; Jer 31.9; Hos 11.1–4).

4   Rom 8.15; Gal 4.6.

5   I believe this phrase was first coined by George Eldon Ladd, a leading Evangelical New Testament scholar of the twentieth century.

6   The Greek word translated here for "temptation" can also mean "testing." We know from James 1.12 that God doesn't tempt anyone. Therefore, it may be a request to be delivered from the evil one or to be spared testing that might overwhelm one's faith.

7   The Greek word used in the text is usually translated "friend" and implies intimate friendship rather than a casual neighbor. Frederick William Danker, "φίλος," *BDAG*, 1058–59.

8   The Greek text of this story creates a bit of a challenge in interpretation, since it is not clear whether the reason the householder gets out of bed and gives his friend the food he requests is because of his own concern about the shame that would be created by not fulfilling the request or if he is responding to the "shameless audacity" of the friend making the request, since he is ignoring proper conventions by knocking on his door at such an inconvenient hour. Many translators have taken it as the audacity of the requesting neighbor, since in the following verse, Jesus tells his disciples to ask, seek, and knock, because the door will be opened to them (11.9). Either way will drive the point home; however, it would seem that in the context the emphasis is placed on the willingness of God to respond to prayer rather than the impudence of the person requesting.

9   This story of the inopportune friend is unique to Luke's Gospel; however, the comparison that follows between God and earthly fathers is also found in Matthew. The final question in Matthew reads, "If you, then, though you are evil, know how to give good gifts to your children, how much more will your Father in heaven give *good gifts* to those who ask him!" (7.11 italics mine). Luke's emphasis on the Holy Spirit in both the life and ministry of Jesus and

later the disciples, probably explains the difference in his Gospel. He has concluded that the good gifts of the Father is the promised Holy Spirit which is described as a gift in Acts 1.4.

10 Frederick William Danker, "ἀντίδικος," *BDAG*, 88.

11 So the NIV, TNIV, NRSV and NASB.

12 Frederick William Danker, "ὑπωπιάζω," *BDAG*, 1043.

CHAPTER SEVEN

CLOTHED WITH POWER

FROM ON HIGH

In 1993, my wife and I attended a church conference where the evening's keynote speaker was Mark Rutland, who was, at that time, pastor of Calvary Assembly of God in Orlando, Florida. At Calvary Assembly, Rutland took a struggling and financially strapped church and turned it into one of the largest of the Assemblies of God fellowship, USA. God had miraculously brought Rutland out of suicidal depression to a powerful Spirit-filled ministry. By 1993, Rutland had also been involved extensively in mission work around the world conducting evangelistic crusades and seeing incredible miracles.

As part of Rutland's evangelistic endeavors, he had made a number of trips to Mexico assisting Jim and Helen Mann, who served as missionaries to Mexico. That evening of the conference, Rutland shared a nearly unbelievable miracle that occurred on one of his trips to Mexico. Rutland was traveling in Mexico with some American pastors, the Mann's, his father-in-law, and an interpreter. The Mann's, at this point, had limited ability in conversational Spanish, so an interpreter was necessary for sermon delivery.

The group had planned a trek to a small village in a remote part of

Mexico to conduct an evening evangelistic service. The American group traveled by bus to this remote location, and had arranged for an interpreter from the nearby village of Tampico to meet them for the service. Rutland and his group arrived at the village, but the interpreter never did. (Rutland learned later that the bus from Tampico had broken down, which prevented the interpreter from arriving.) Recognizing their limited ability to speak Spanish, the group managed, with some difficulty, to communicate to the local pastor that he would have to preach the sermon, since their interpreter had not arrived.

Rutland decided that he would, before the Mexican pastor's sermon, stand up and greet the congregation with the few Spanish phrases he had picked up during his travels. As he began to speak, Rutland realized that phrase after phrase kept coming to his mind. Thirty-five minutes later, he had preached his first sermon in Spanish! During the sermon, everyone in the small Mexican congregation began to realize that a miracle was taking place right in front of them. At one point during the sermon, Rutland's father-in-law stood up in the back row and said, "What are you doing?" Rutland answered, "It's the Lord! Something's going on! It's a miracle, I think." Rutland's father-in-law, who was not yet a believer, came to the Lord that evening and returned to Tallahassee, Florida, where he joined a local Pentecostal congregation.

Rutland told us that his ability to speak Spanish has never left him. To demonstrate, he spoke several phrases in fluent Spanish to the conference attendees, the accuracy of which was affirmed by the delightful cheers of that evening's Hispanic attendees.[1] This miracle is just one of many that Rutland reports in his autobiography and is just one among thousands that have occurred over the years in the ministries of God's people around the world. Rutland attributes the power and dramatic turnaround in his own life and ministry to the baptism in the Holy Spirit,[2] and his testimony is echoed by countless others within the Pentecostal/Charismatic renewal of the past century.

The Baptism in the Holy Spirit

The phrase, "baptism in the Holy Spirit," used by Rutland and many other Pentecostals and Charismatics never appears in the New Testament. It probably derives from Jesus's own command to his disciples, "Do not leave Jerusalem, but wait for the gift my Father promised, which you have heard me speak about. For John baptized with water, but in a few days you will be *baptized with the Holy Spirit*" (Acts 1.4–5; cf. Lk 3.16 italics mine).

This command of Jesus affirms what John the Baptist himself had said concerning Jesus in Luke 3.16 that he will "baptize you with the Holy Spirit." While Luke never calls the arrival of the promised Holy Spirit the "baptism in the Holy Spirit," he does often refer to believers being "full of" or "filled with the Holy Spirit."[3] When contemporary Pentecostals and Charismatics refer to the "baptism in the Holy Spirit," this is what they most often mean—a life characterized by the fullness of the Spirit that empowers believers to be effective disciples and carry on the ministry of Jesus as the first believers did.

In the contemporary church, there are many different views on what being "filled with the Spirit" means, how it is evidenced, and when it happens. My intention is not to enter into a lengthy theological debate, because this book is about discipleship, particularly from Luke's point of view. Most Lukan scholars recognize Luke's thematic emphasis on the role of the Holy Spirit in both Jesus's and his disciples' lives and ministries. It is my intention to highlight this emphasis and to demonstrate how the presence and power of the Holy Spirit, what Luke calls being "full of the Holy Spirit," was and is indispensable for Jesus's disciples both then and now.

Luke's Emphasis on the Holy Spirit

We have discussed earlier in this book Luke's emphasis on the role of the Holy Spirit in the life and ministry of Jesus; but I think a restatement of some of the evidence is in order to set the tone for the current discussion. It isn't that the other Gospels don't mention the Holy Spirit; but similar to how we demonstrated with the theme of prayer, Luke narrates the Holy Spirit into the telling of the life of Jesus in ways that are unique to Luke's Gospel. Luke agrees with Matthew that Jesus was conceived by the Holy Spirit and with both Matthew and Mark that the Holy Spirit descended on Jesus at his baptism. It is, however, in Luke's unique and lengthy telling of the annunciation and births of both Jesus and John the Baptist that his emphasis begins to stand out.

In the first two chapters of Luke's Gospel, the Spirit is mentioned seven times and often through the use of Luke's preferred phrase, "full of the Holy Spirit." The citing of the Spirit is not just in connection with Jesus, but also in connection with other characters in the story. For example, the angel Gabriel says that John the Baptist will be "filled with the Spirit" from his mother's womb (1.15). When Mary visits Elizabeth, Elizabeth is said to be "filled with the Holy Spirit" (1.41) at the greeting of Mary, and she begins to prophesy. Mary in turn does the same, as Luke records what is called "Mary's Song" or "Mary's *Magnificat*" (1.46–55). Zechariah too, upon the birth of John the Baptist, is "filled with the Holy Spirit" and prophesies (1.67).

Eight days after Jesus's birth, his parents take him to the temple where he is to be circumcised, and we, once again, see two prophetic figures enter the story. Simeon, who is described as a "righteous and devout man," who had the Holy Spirit "on him," is "moved by the Spirit" to enter the temple courts at the precise time Jesus is being presented to the Lord. Simeon, Luke tells us, had been promised that he would not die before he sees the "Lord's Messiah." Upon seeing the child, he begins to prophesy over him to his parents. Similarly, Anna, a widow of the tribe of Asher, is also in the temple fasting and praying, when she too begins to prophesy over the child to everyone who is looking for the hope of Israel (2.25–38).

All four Gospels attest to the descent of the Spirit at Jesus's baptism and, according to the Synoptic Gospels, subsequently take him into the wilderness for forty days of temptation by Satan. However, it is Luke who uniquely records that Jesus, "full of the Holy Spirit," left the Jordan to enter the wilderness and that Jesus returned to Galilee from the wilderness "in the power of the Spirit" (Lk 4.1, 14). Upon Jesus's return, he enters the Nazareth synagogue where he announces, "The Spirit of the Lord is on me" (Lk 4.18; Isa 61.1) to proclaim the good news to the poor, freedom for the captives, recovery of sight for the blind and to announce the time of God's favor. This unique scene in Nazareth serves the same function as the one in Acts 2 on the Day of Pentecost—to demonstrate that both Jesus's and his disciples' ministries are Spirit-empowered.

References to the Holy Spirit diminish in the rest of Luke's Gospel but will return in significant numbers in the narrative of Acts, as Jesus's followers carry forward his ministry. References to the Spirit in the Gospel, however, are no longer necessary, as the foundation has been laid for his assumed presence throughout Jesus's ministry. Luke demonstrates within the first four chapters of his Gospel that God has remembered his covenant made with Abraham and is visiting his people through the long-anticipated promised Messiah. The coming of the Messiah to Israel, so keenly celebrated in the prophetic words of Mary, Elizabeth, Zechariah, Simeon, and Anna, also means the restoration of the Spirit of prophecy to God's people. The Holy Spirit is the Spirit of prophecy, who fills his people with inspired utterances for the glory of God. Luke introduces this concept through these early characters in the Gospel and confirms it through the Joel prophecy of Peter's Acts 2 speech.

The Joel 2.28–32 prophecy, as recorded in Acts 2, displays Luke's editing hand through minor enhancements Luke has made to the quotation. These enhancements highlight key points in the prophecy that are paradigmatic for the Acts narrative. Two of these editorial points are the addition of the phrase, "and they will prophesy," in 2.18, and the word "signs" added to the phrase, "I will show wonders in the heavens above and *signs* on the earth below," found in Acts 2.19 (italics mine).

The Joel prophecy of the Hebrew[4] text reads, "I will show wonders in the heavens and on the earth." Luke is not changing the prophecy into something more or less than what it is but is providing emphases on aspects that what he will demonstrate are being fulfilled through Jesus's disciples by the presence of the Holy Spirit in their lives.[5] The prominence of prophetic speech, what we will call inspired speech, and of "signs and wonders," is evident throughout the Acts narrative.

Inspired Speech

The connection between the Spirit and inspired speech in Luke-Acts is an important element that ties the two narratives together and is also significant for the overall message that Luke wishes to convey. As already noted, Luke sees the return of the Spirit to God's people as a fulfillment of Old Testament prophecy. Joel is not the only prophet to predict this move of God, so does Ezekiel (11.19; 36.26–27; 39.29). However, Luke reaches even further back to Moses for his inspiration. Twice in Acts, Luke makes reference to Moses's words concerning a prophet, who will arise in Israel like himself, and the people must listen to him (Acts 3.22; 7.37; Deut 18.14–19). Moses's declaration in Deuteronomy is interpreted by Luke as a prophetic word for the true prophet or Messiah that God will send. Remember, Luke portrays Jesus in the guise of a prophet like Moses, Elijah, and Elisha (two of whom he meets on the Mount of Transfiguration) but eventually reveals him as more than a prophet. He is the Son of God.

In addition, Luke seems to favor another Torah passage found in Numbers 11.24–30. According to this story, the burden of leading God's people has become too much for Moses, and God agrees, in an effort to ease Moses's burden, to place on seventy of Israel's elders a portion of the Spirit that rests on Moses. Moses gathers the elders before the Tent of Meeting at which time God takes of the Spirit on Moses and places it on the elders. Upon receiving the Spirit, the elders begin to prophesy. Joshua, Moses's aid, learns that two of the elders, who had not reported to the Tent of Meeting, are prophesying out in the camp. Joshua, who is apparently concerned for Moses's unique position as God's prophetic leader, implores Moses to make them stop. Moses replies, "I wish that all the Lord's people were prophets and that the Lord would put his Spirit on them!" (11.29).

The correlation between this Number's passage and Luke's Gospel is found in the account of Jesus's sending of the seventy-two (or seventy)[6] on mission in Luke 10.1–24. This is a separate sending from that of the Twelve in Luke 9.1–6 (notice seventy-two "others" in 10.1). Jesus is once again portrayed in the guise of a prophet like Moses, who gives his power to this larger group of disciples in order that they might carry out the same mission to which he is called. Through this scene, uniquely recorded in Luke's Gospel, Luke appears to be suggesting that Moses's wish, expressed in Numbers 11.29, is being fulfilled through Jesus's ministry. This happens not only in the sending of the seventy-two but ultimately through the impartation of his Spirit on the Day of Pentecost, by which he creates one prophetic people for God.

When I speak of a "prophetic people," I am using the terms "prophetic" and "prophecy" more broadly than simply foretelling the future. In fact, foretelling is only a part of biblical prophecy. Prophecy is more broadly the proclamation of the words of God, or "forthtelling," done under the inspiration of the Holy Spirit. This is what I call inspired speech, and it comes in a variety of forms. Such inspired speech comes in the form of the declaration of the praises and exploits of God, such as what Mary and Zechariah do in their prophetic songs. Prophecy also comes in the form of prophetic witness, as when Peter, "full of the Holy Spirit," testifies boldly before the Sanhedrin (Acts 4.8–12) or Stephen refutes his opponents with "the wisdom the Spirit gave him as he spoke" (Acts 6.10). However, prophecy can still take the form of prediction, as when Agabus foretells a famine in Judea (Acts 11.27–28) or Paul's arrest in Jerusalem (Acts 21.10–11). God has, in fulfillment of Numbers 11.29, created for himself a people, full of his Spirit, empowered to speak in his name. The church is God's prophetic people.

Acts also presents us with another form of inspired speech called speaking in tongues. Speaking in tongues under the inspiration of the Holy Spirit appears first on the Day of Pentecost but is repeated again on other occasions, when believers encounter the fullness of the Spirit (Acts 10.46; 19.6). The Day of Pentecost is, however, somewhat unique compared to the other Act's accounts of speaking in tongues, as these tongues were heard and understood by the crowd gathered that day in Jerusalem.

The Day of Pentecost, also known as the Festival of Weeks, is one of several Jewish pilgrimage feasts, which means that Jerusalem was crowded with Jews from all over the known world. Luke pauses in the narrative to list just how many areas of the world are represented by the crowd and how each heard in their own language the praises of God (Acts 2.5–11). This emphasis on the international nature of the Pentecost event underlines the universality of the Gospel message and the church's mission (Acts 1.8). The association of tongues, or inspired speech, with the praise of God in international languages and Peter's subsequent explanation through Joel that this is evidence of God creating a prophetic people, aligns tongues and prophecy together as signs that God, "in the last days," has poured out his Spirit on "all flesh."[7]

Full of the Holy Spirit

As noted earlier in this chapter, Luke's preferred phrase for the presence of the Holy Spirit in the lives of the believers is to be "full of (or filled with) the Holy Spirit." As demonstrated, this phrase is found several times early in Luke's Gospel, and it is in turn found frequently in the Acts narrative. It is just another way that Luke laces his two-volume work together, showing that the inauguration of the messianic age is characterized by the presence of the Spirit in the lives of Jesus and his followers. Inspired speech also plays a part in this union of the two narratives; in fact, inspired speech and being filled with the Spirit seem to go hand in hand for Luke. People who are "full of the Holy Spirit," like Elizabeth and Zechariah or Peter and Stephen, speak out the praises of God or testify boldly to the work of God. Being "full of the Holy Spirit" is not the right of any particular people group, as Luke portrays both men and women and Jews and Gentiles as having this experience.

The fact that Jesus and his disciples begin their ministries "full of the

Holy Spirit" (Lk 4.1; Acts 2.4) is important for Luke's narrative and for our topic. The purpose of discipleship is to become like one's master. Jesus states at one point in his teaching of the disciples that "The student is not above the teacher, but everyone who is fully trained will be like their teacher" (6.40). Jesus has invested in his disciples through his teaching on obedience, possessions, prayer, faith, and self-denial. He has sent them on mission with the authority to conduct a ministry like his own, and they survived his traumatic crucifixion and are astounded at his resurrection. However, one element in their preparation to be his witnesses still remains. In his final instruction to his disciples, Jesus says, "I am going to send you what my Father has promised; but stay in the city until you have been clothed with power from on high" (Lk24.49).

"Clothed with power from on high" is just another way of expressing what it means to be "full of the Holy Spirit." The Spirit, who will wrap the disciples in power like a garment, will reside in them and work through them in the demonstration of "signs and wonders." This latter expression, which Luke adopts from his adapted version of Joel's prophecy, is found in various forms throughout the Acts narrative,[8] as Jesus's disciples carry on a ministry like his. However, instead of the Isa 61.1–2 prophecy being paradigmatic for their ministry as it was for Jesus's, for them, it is the Joel prophecy. It is the empowering of the Spirit, the "fullness" of the Spirit, which will enable them to follow their Master in mission and live out the life of a true disciple. As is intimated at one point in Acts, the Holy Spirit poured out at Pentecost is indeed the "Spirit of Jesus" (Acts 16.7), and he lives in resurrection power through the replicated lives of his followers, the "Christ-ians" (Acts 11.26c).

Luke goes to some length to demonstrate that the ministry and lives of Jesus's disciples duplicate those of their teacher. The two main characters that stand out in the book of Acts are Peter and Paul. Peter, who is portrayed in both the Gospel and Acts as the lead apostle, is the only individual apostle to whom speech is accredited in Acts. Paul is presented as the leader of the gentile mission.

The approval of the gentile mission by both the Jerusalem leadership and the lead apostle Peter is important to Luke. The significance of their approval is demonstrated through the literary prominence given to the story of Peter's vision of unclean animals and his subsequent visit to Cornelius's house in Acts 10. This account is told and retold a total of three times in Acts. Peter retells the event as justification of his visit to a gentile's home before the Jerusalem elders (Acts 11.4–17) and again during his defense of gentile inclusion at the Jerusalem Council (Acts 15.7–9). Peter's role in Acts eventually diminishes in favor of Paul, the Apostle to the Gentiles, who leads the gentile mission from Acts 13 onward.

Although Paul was not an original follower of Jesus, both his and Peter's lives and ministries are portrayed as emulating that of Jesus. Reminiscent of Jesus's ministry, Luke writes concerning Peter and the other apostles, "Crowds gathered also from the towns around Jerusalem, bringing their sick and those tormented by impure spirits, and all of them were healed" (Acts 5.16; cf. Lk 4.40–41). In addition, Peter describes Jesus as having been "accredited by God to you by miracles, wonders and signs" (Acts 2.22), and later Luke reports similarly that "Everyone was filled with awe at the many wonders and signs performed by the apostles" (Acts 2.43).

In Acts 9.32–43, Peter performs two miracles similar to those of Jesus. The first miracle is the healing of the paralytic Aeneas, who is described as a man who "had been bedridden for eight years." Peter, like Jesus to the paralytic of Luke 5, heals Aeneas and tells him to get up and take up his mat. The second miracle is similar to the raising of Jairus's daughter in Luke 8.51–56. Peter raises a disciple named Tabitha (also Dorcas) from the dead. In similar fashion as Jesus, he put everyone out of the room, prayed, and then said to her, "Tabitha, get up." Like Jairus's daughter, Tabitha sat up and Peter helped her to her feet.

Paul in turn is also portrayed as one who walks in "the way" with Jesus. A large portion of Paul's story in Acts has to do with Paul on trial, and it is interesting to note how Paul's court trials parallel Jesus's in a number of ways. For example, in similar fashion as Jesus, who predicts his suffering and death in Jerusalem three times, Paul is warned three times that trials and hardships await him as he journeys up to Jerusalem. While on trial, again like Jesus who stood before the Jewish authorities, the Roman procurator Pontius Pilate, and Herod Antipas, Paul stands before the Jewish authorities, the Roman procurator Porcius Festus, and the Jewish King Herod Agrippa. Other similarities could be mentioned, but these suffice to establish the pattern which demonstrates that these disciples have joined Jesus on the way and have become like their teacher. The fullness of the Spirit brings about this transformation, who is the promised gift of the Father.

A Promise and a Gift

Jesus tells his disciples in Luke 24.49 that "I am going to send you what my Father has *promised*," which is reiterated in Acts 1.4 when he says, "But wait for the *gift* my Father *promised*" (italics mine). These two verses serve to unite the two narratives and allow the reader to pick up where the last book left off. What is interesting about these two verses is the characterization of the coming Spirit as a "promise" and a "gift" of the Father. These words are no doubt a reference to the proclamations of the Hebrew prophets, in which God promised one day to place his Spirit in his people.

The presence of the Spirit will be the sign that a new covenant has been established with God's people, through which he removes their heart of stone and replaces it with a heart of flesh (Ezek 11.19–20; Jer 31.31–34). If we had any doubts about the origin of this promise, Luke does not leave us clueless as Peter's speech on the Day of Pentecost affirms its prophetic origins and announces once again that this gift and "promise is for you and your children and for all who are far off—for all whom the Lord our God will call" (2.39).

As the Acts narrative develops beyond the Day of Pentecost, "gift" becomes the working definition for the Spirit. In Acts 8.20, Peter rebukes Simon the Sorcerer because he attempts to buy the "gift of God with money." Again, in Cornelius's house, the believers are astonished that "the gift of the Holy Spirit is poured out even on the Gentiles" (10.45); and in Peter's defense of the Cornelius event he tells the Jerusalem elders, "God gave them the same gift that he gave us" (11.17).

The understanding that the Spirit is a gift to God's people is clearly in Luke's mind, even when writing the Gospel. As mentioned in the chapter on prayer, Luke's record of Jesus's teaching on prayer climaxes with this statement, "If you being evil know how to give good gifts to your children, how much more will your Father in heaven give *the Holy Spirit* to those who ask him!" (11.13 italics mine).

This same teaching is also found in Matthew's Gospel, where Jesus's teaching climaxes with a similar statement but with one important difference, "how much more will your Father in heaven give *good gifts* to those who ask him!" (Mt 7.11 italics mine). Luke has interpreted Jesus's teaching to speak more precisely about the Holy Spirit and indicates to us that in his understanding, the Holy Spirit is a good gift, perhaps the greatest gift, God gives to his disciples.

I emphasize these two terms, "promise" and "gift," because I think they are important for us to embrace as contemporary disciples. Both terms emphasize the faithfulness and grace of God. Jesus understood that the ability to live out his teachings, and to carry on the ministry he left to his disciples, would require the same power that characterized his ministry. They would have to be "full of the Holy Spirit" just as he was. The presence of the Holy Spirit would also mark his disciples, the people of God, as a prophetic people, who would speak forth the words of God with boldness and perform signs and wonders to confirm that word.

Two-thousand years later, the promise and gift still remain. God is still filling his people with the Holy Spirit. Of course, over that period the church has grown globally and has become theologically diverse on a number of issues, including the role of the Holy Spirit in the life of a believer. At one end of the spectrum are those who believe that Spirit-empowered signs and wonders, which characterized the church of Acts, have ceased and were only necessary at the beginning in order to establish the church. The presence of the written Scriptures and established church doctrine is now sufficient to sustain the faith.

On the opposite end are the Pentecostals and Charismatics who believe that the Spirit-inspired phenomena recorded in Acts are still possible, available, necessary, and happening in the contemporary church. Both groups, and everyone in between, would generally accept that the Holy Spirit is present and at work in the church and more specifically in the lives of believers; but the purpose and manner in which his presence is manifested would be the points of contention.

Personal Experience

At the beginning of this chapter, I expressed disinterest in embarking on a major theological debate about the many issues that are involved in a discussion of the purpose and manner in which the Holy Spirit operates in the believer today. That is not the purpose of this book and would bog down the overall thrust toward our goal of understanding Luke's presentation of discipleship. Clearly, Luke sees the Holy Spirit as an indispensable part of both Jesus's ministry and the subsequent ministry of his disciples. The presence of the Holy Spirit is what makes the disciples "like their teacher."

Every true believer has the presence of the Holy Spirit in their lives. However, Luke does demonstrate to us that there is a dimension of his presence, which he calls being "full of the Holy Spirit," that seems to be characterized by inspired speech and the ability to perform signs and wonders in support of the gospel message. As a Pentecostal, I do believe that such power is available to every follower of Jesus. I have experienced this fullness of the Spirit and I know many others have as well. I believe that the reality of this truth is why the Pentecostal movement worldwide is the one of the fastest-growing movements within Christendom.[9]

I have taught undergraduate students for many years, primarily at a private Pentecostal university. I encounter students all the time who struggle with understanding and accepting the fullness of the Spirit, as it is often described in my tradition, and other students who readily embrace it. I have been a part of the Classical Pentecostal[10] movement all of my life, and in this movement, it has widely been accepted that speaking in tongues is the evidence that one has experienced the fullness of the Spirit. Indeed, this is the most prevalent result when believers receive the fullness of the Spirit in Acts, but it is not the only result. In one instance, they spoke in tongues *and* prophesied (Acts 19), and at other times no specific evidence is mentioned at all (Acts 8.15–17; 9.17–18), although it can be inferred.

All Pentecostals don't accept that tongues is *the* evidence of the fullness of the Spirit, but most do accept that the presence of the Spirit in the life of a believer results in some kind of supernatural manifestation or empowerment. When I encounter students who are wrestling with all of these issues, I simply share my own experience, which in the end is the best I can offer beyond Scriptural evidence or theological doctrine. So, to end this chapter, I offer to you my experience.

I shared in the first chapter how I came to know Christ and in the previous chapter how my walk of discipleship began to be fleshed out, albeit with a bumpy start. After getting my relationship with Christ back on track, I pursued that relationship with all my heart. Having been raised in the Pentecostal tradition, I was always told that beyond salvation there was another experience often called "the baptism in the Holy Spirit," which I will call in the language of Luke being "full of the Spirit." I was also told that I would know if I had been filled with the Spirit, by the evidence of speaking in tongues. So, I began looking for and expecting this experience in my own life.

I actually didn't experience the "fullness of the Spirit" for some time after salvation. It wasn't for lack of desire, and the fact that I wasn't experiencing what I was told to expect greatly frustrated me. It didn't make me angry that I was not receiving this fullness of the Spirit, but I was hungry and I wanted all that God had for me.

Pentecostals often used to talk about "tarrying" at the church altar for the Holy Spirit to fill us. That was just another way of saying that one needed to "wait" for the experience, but we should be assured that God wanted to give it to us as it is a "gift" from him. Of course, this idea of "tarrying" or "waiting" came from the Luke-Acts texts where Jesus told his disciples to wait until they were clothed with power from on high. There was much instruction and advice from "old timers" about what to expect and how to receive this fullness. Still, I remained frustrated.

I waited at the altar in prayer like I was told. I sought advice from trusted friends, and I cried out to God in my own private prayer times. I remember one evening, while praying privately, I was looking at 1 Cor 14.1 where Paul says, "Desire spiritual gifts, but rather that [you] may prophecy" (KJV). I said to the Lord, "Maybe speaking in tongues isn't for everyone; so I ask you for the gift of prophecy."

One thing I knew from what Paul said, from what Luke said, and from what everyone around me was saying is that the Holy Spirit is a gift given by God; and according to Paul, this same Holy Spirit distributed gifts to the body as he wills (1 Cor 12.4). Since these things are gifts and the Bible says to desire them, I figured God would give them to someone as desirous as me. I didn't know, until later, the impact that simple prayer would have on my life.

At that time, I began attending a small group meeting hosted by a family in my church. One evening after Bible study, we went to prayer as we normally did. Most of our prayer times in the group meetings were unstructured and fairly open-ended, but one thing that was true of all that attended is that we were hungry for a closer walk with God. One evening during the prayer time, I was on my knees praying, when I heard a voice in my head say, "Open your mouth and I will fill it with good things." I recognized the phrase as echoing a Bible verse I had read in Psalm 81.10, and so, in obedience, I turned my face toward heaven and opened my mouth.

Immediately the Holy Spirit came on me with such power that the force of his presence picked me up and gently laid me on the floor. I felt power all over me as if I had been "clothed with power from on high"! I immediately began speaking in unintelligible tongues and continued to do that all through the evening, as well as delivering several prophetic messages in my native language to the group. That night, God had not only allowed me to speak in tongues but also to prophesy. I had gotten all I had asked!

The prayer language I received that evening has stayed with me for the past forty plus years, and I have on several occasions not only delivered prophetic words, but I have also experienced other gifts from the Holy Spirit, which Paul talks about in 1 Cor 12. I learned, that evening, several things about God. One, God is a benevolent God, who fulfills his promises and gives good gifts to his children. Two, God hears our prayers and honors our desire to draw closer to him in order to have all that he has promised us. Three, this promise and gift is truly "for you and your children and for all who are far off—for all whom the Lord our God will call" (Acts 2.39).

I don't know why it took more than a year before I had this experience, and I am sure the time frame is different for everyone. Maybe it was my lack of faith. I can't say. What I can say is what I have already said—God honors every hungry heart and hears every sincere prayer. The fourth and final thing I have learned is that joining Jesus on the way involves all of the things we have discussed in this book, but the ability to have a successful journey, and truly to emulate the Master, requires being "clothed with power from on high."

1   The details of this story come from personal experience, Rutland's autobi-
    ography, *Launch Out into the Deep* (Lexington, KY: Bristol Books, 1987),
    69–70; and Jordan Daniel May, "'In Our Tongues': A Defense of Miraculous
    Speech Based on Eyewitness Testimony," *EJ* (2015): n. p., url: http://enrich-
    mentjournal.ag.org/201501/201501_010_Tongues.cfm.

2   Rutland, *Launch Out*, 31–33.

3   See Acts 2.4; 4.8, 31; 6.3, 5; 7.55; 9.17; 11.24; 13.9; 13.52.

4   Luke is most likely using the Greek translation of the Hebrew text called
    the Septuagint (LXX), but both the Greek and Hebrew agree at this point. It
    should be noted here, as well, that both the Hebrew and Greek texts number
    Joel 2.28–32 as 3.1–5.

5   This is not the only editing that takes place under Luke's hand, but the ones
    that are significant for our discussion. For a fuller discussion, see Robert P.
    Menzies, *Pentecost: This is Our Story* (Springfield: Gospel Publishing House,
    2013), 77–80.

6   The Greek manuscripts vary on whether the number is 70 or 72. The majority
    of manuscripts have, but the better manuscripts have 72 and is the number
    favored by scholars. Both numbers actually carry symbolism in a variety of
    ways. In Genesis 10 of the Hebrew text, there are 70 nations descended from
    Noah's sons and 72 in the Greek text (LXX). The reference to the nations
    would be enough to give Luke symbolic connection. For a fuller discussion
    of the literary background and symbolism of Luke 10, see John T. Carroll,
    Luke: A Commentary, NTL (Louisville: Westminster John Knox, 2012),
    231, n. a. Also, Joel B. Green, *The Gospel of Luke*, NINTC (Grand Rapids:
    Eerdmans, 1997), 409–11. For the connection between Numbers 11 and the
    sending of the 72, see Menzies, *Pentecost*, 31–5.

7   Menzies, *Pentecost*, 74–7, calls tongues a type of prophecy. I would use the
    more general expression, "inspired speech," but tongues can be prophetic,
    when interpreted as on the Day of Pentecost (cf. 1 Cor 14.5).

8   For the use of "signs" and "wonders" in Acts, see 2.22 (connected to Jesus),
    43; 4.30; 5.12; 6.8; 7.36 (connected to Moses); 14.3; 15.12 (connected to the
    gentile mission).

9   A number of studies have been done on the growth of the Pentecostal movement worldwide. It is sometimes difficult, however, to get accurate statistics, but most researchers accept that the Pentecostal/Charismatic or renewal movement, particularly in the global south, is one of the fastest-growing. Here is a study done by the Pew Research Foundation, https://www.pewresearch.org/wp-content/uploads/sites/7/2006/10/pentecostals-08.pdf. For more dynamic and up-to-date information, see http://www.atlasofpentecostalism.net.

10   Classical Pentecostals are those who usually belong to denominations that trace their roots back to the Azusa Street revival of 1906. Menzies, *Pentecost*, 13, provides a helpful breakdown of the many classifications of groups within the Pentecostal renewal movement.

CONCLUSION

THE JOURNEY CONTINUES

We have spent most of our time in the travel narrative of Luke's Gospel, where Luke uses the context of Jesus's journey from Galilee to Jerusalem as a framework on which to hang most of Jesus's discipleship teaching. We have come to understand that this journey motif serves equally well as a metaphor for the journey to which Jesus calls all of his disciples. We are all called to join him on the way—the way to the cross.

The travel narrative ends with Jesus's triumphal entry into Jerusalem, which is soon followed by his crucifixion. Given this scenario, I thought at one point, "The Journey Ends" would be an appropriate title for the conclusion of this book. Upon further reflection, however, I realize that the cross is not the end of Jesus's journey. We as human beings often think of death as the end, but actually for those in Christ, it is not an end at all. For Jesus, it was certainly not the end. Jesus, as he predicted, rose to life again three days after his crucifixion. Death was not a defeat for him but a victory. He conquered death, hell, and the grave for all of us, so that death does not have to be an end but the beginning of a new life in him.

This truth of death to life was brought home to me in a very real way while writing this book. You may recall that I stated in the introductory chapter that the writing of this book is for me as much about helping others in their pursuit of Jesus as it is about my own journey. In the final months of writing, my wife and I began to face some important changes in our life and ministry together that necessitated discerning God's new direction for us. In response, we spent some time fasting and praying to help us better hear God's voice.

At that time, I happened to be reading Richard Foster's book, *Prayer: Finding the Heart's True Home*.[1] Foster has a chapter called, "The Prayer of Relinquishment,"[2] in which he discusses moments in our lives we are called to give back to God something that is very precious to us, either tangible or intangible. It isn't that God is "mean" or "sadistic" simply demanding from his children their most precious possessions. Rather, it is often our will and our desire to control that hinders us from receiving the best God has for us. Foster explains that we relinquish the things most dear to us to have something far greater from God. We are after the treasures of the kingdom, not the treasures of this life. Foster writes, "Relinquishment brings to us a priceless treasure: *the crucifixion of the will*."[3]

On the last day of our fasting time, I told my wife that I felt as if I needed a spiritual breakthrough. I can't really explain how that felt, but I knew there was something I was missing that I believed God was asking of me. As we went to prayer, God began to remind me of Foster's chapter on "the prayer of relinquishment." I remembered the prime example Foster gave of this type of prayer was Jesus in the Garden of Gethsemane where Jesus prayed, "Not my will, but yours be done." I suddenly felt as if God was asking me to do the same—to give my life up completely to him and allow him to be in control.

Out of obedience, I prayed that prayer of Jesus—the prayer of relinquishment. It was terribly frightening to say those words—"not my will, but yours be done." Letting go is not easy for me. I like to be in control and death, whether physical or to self, seems so terrifying. That was the hardest prayer I have ever prayed, but it was worth it. I have experienced such joy since that moment, and I have felt more alive than ever before. I realize that by praying that prayer of relinquishment, I gave up my life, my control, and God gave me new life—a better life. Out of death to self came life.

Foster says that when we pray the prayer of relinquishment, God often will give back the very thing we give up.[4]Foster does caution, however, that getting back what we give up is not always the result of the prayer of relinquishment, but in the case of discipleship, I think it is. When Jesus told his disciples, "whoever wants to be my disciple must deny themselves and take up their cross daily and follow me" (Lk 9.23), he was teaching them about relinquishment. He was teaching them the very thing that he was doing and would do in the Garden of Gethsemane.

A principle of the kingdom is that we must give up to God what we actually wish to keep. As Jesus said to his disciples in the very next verse, "For whoever wants to save their life will lose it, but whoever loses their life for me will save it" (Lk 9.24). This is one of the paradoxes of the kingdom and very difficult for us to grasp. Understanding comes only through a work of the Spirit in our lives. It is counterintuitive to try to save one's life through losing it. However, when we relinquish our lives into the hands of the author of life—the one who can bring life out of death—he gives us back lives worth living.

Surrendering ourselves to God is the essence of discipleship. Once we have done this, then our obedience, our possessions, our family responsibilities, and all our worldly obligations fall into line. Death to self places God in control and offers us the best opportunity to live life to the fullest. Even though Paul didn't accompany Jesus on the dusty roads of Galilee, he sums up well the path of true discipleship. "I have been crucified with Christ and I no longer live, but Christ lives in me. The life I now live in the body, I live by faith in the Son of God, who loved me and gave himself for me" (Gal 2.20). Jesus's invitation to all who follow him is to join him on the way to the cross, but the journey doesn't end there. The journey continues through resurrection to new life in him.

1 Richard J. Foster, *Prayer: Finding the Heart's True Home* (New York: Harper Collins, 1992), 47.

2 Ibid.

3 Ibid, 53 (italics his).

4 Ibid, 52.

If you would like to use *Joining Jesus on the Way:*
Discipleship in the 21st Century as a resource for your small group or
Bible study, you may obtain discussion questions for each chapter by
emailing the author at joiningjesusontheway@gmail.com.

BIBLIOGRAPHY

Bauckham, Richard. *Gospel Women: Studies in the Named Women in the Gospels.* Grand Rapids: Eerdmans, 2002.

Carroll, John T. *Luke: A Commentary.* The New Testament Library. Louisville: Westminster John Knox, 2012.

Daigle, Lauren. "Known to Me." *Guideposts* (Feb 2019). Danbury, CT.

Foster, Richard J. *Prayer: Finding the Heart's True Home.* New York: Harper Collins, 1992.

Green Joel B. *The Gospel of Luke.* New International New Testament Commentary. Grand Rapids: Eerdmans, 1997.

Johnson, Luke Timothy. *Prophetic Jesus, Prophetic Church: The Challenge of Luke-Acts to Contemporary Christians.* Grand Rapids: Eerdmans, 2011.

May, Jordan Daniel. "'In Our Tongues': A Defense of Miraculous Speech Based on Eyewitness Testimony," *Enrichment Journal* (2015): n. p., url: http://enrichmentjournal. ag.org/201501/201501_010_Tongues.cfm

Menzies, Robert P. *Pentecost: This is Our Story.* Springfield, MO: Gospel Publishing House, 2013.

Peterson, Eugene H. *A Long Obedience in the Same Direction: Discipleship in an Instant Society.* Downers Grove: InterVarsity, 1980.

Rutland, Mark. *Launch Out into the Deep.* Lexington, KY: Bristol Books, 1987.

Witherington, III, Ben. *The Acts of the Apostles: A Socio-Rhetorical Commentary.* Grand Rapids: Eerdmans, 1998.

CPSIA information can be obtained
at www.ICGtesting.com
Printed in the USA
LVHW110545251119
638178LV00007B/3/P